LOWE'S
Let's Build Something Together®

creative
ideas
for home and garden®

COLOR

LOWE'S COMPANIES, INC.

Robert Niblock, PRESIDENT, CEO, AND CHAIRMAN
OF THE BOARD

Melissa Birdsong, VICE PRESIDENT, TREND,
DESIGN & BRAND

Mary E. Carpenter, MERCHANDISE DIRECTOR

Bob Gfeller, SENIOR VP, MARKETING

Carol Knuth, VP, MERCHANDISING

Mike Menser, SENIOR VP, GENERAL MERCHANDISE
MANAGER

Larry D. Stone, SENIOR EXECUTIVE VP,
MERCHANDISING AND MARKETING

Sandy Culver, CUSTOMER RELATIONSHIP MANAGER

Anne Serafin, MERCHANDISING DIRECTOR

CREATIVE IDEAS FOR HOME & GARDEN: COLOR

Stephanie Patton, VP, SPC CUSTOM PUBLISHING

Catherine Hall, ACCOUNT DIRECTOR, SPC CUSTOM
PUBLISHING

Shane Jordan, ACCOUNT MANAGER, SPC CUSTOM
PUBLISHING

Sally W. Smith, EDITOR

Lisa Stockwell, WRITER

Alice Lankford Elmore and Kelly Margaret Smith,
CONSULTING EDITORS

Christine Rocha/Hespenheide Design, DESIGN AND
PAGE PRODUCTION

John Edmonds, COPY EDITOR

Sheryl Jones and Ryan Kelly, PRODUCTION EDITORS

Mary Roybal, PROOFREADER

Randy Miyake, ILLUSTRATOR

Nanette Cardon, INDEXER

Linda Bouchard, PRODUCTION SPECIALIST

10 9 8 7 6 5 4 3 2 1

First Printing February 2007.

ISBN-13: 978-0-376-00926-5
ISBN-10: 0-376-00926-8

Library of Congress Control Number: 2006932837.

Printed in the United States of America.

For additional copies of *Creative Ideas for Home &
Garden: Color* or any other Lowe's book, visit
www.sunsetbooks.com or call 1-800-526-5111.

Cover: Complementary red and green in mid-tones and deep tones (see pages 78–101) warm up stainless steel appliances in this kitchen. Photo: Geoffrey Nilsen.

Page 1: Pattern enlivens this blue-green study (see pages 14–15 to learn about the effects of light, pattern, and texture on color). Photo: E. Andrew McKinney.

Above: Bright colors (see pages 102–125) are often playful. Photo: John O'Hagan.

Notes for Readers: Because of the limitations of the printing process, colors printed in this book may not be an exact representation of a specified paint or fabric. Check paint chips at Lowe's for the true colors. If you like the color on the page better than the one on the paint chip, a Lowe's paint specialist can mix a match for you. Items shown in the photos may not be available at Lowe's, but visit the store to find a similar product that will achieve the look you like.

Almost any do-it-yourself project involves a risk of some sort. Your tools, materials, and skills will vary, as will the conditions at your project site. Lowe's Companies, Inc., and its subsidiaries ("Lowe's") have made every effort to be complete and accurate in the instructions and other content in this publication. However, neither Lowe's nor the publisher will assume any responsibility or liability for damages or losses sustained or incurred in the course of your home-improvement or repair project or in the course of your use of the item you create or repair. Always follow manufacturer's operating instructions in the use of tools, check and follow your local building codes, and observe all standard safety precautions.

Let's Build Something Together....

Color is a wonderful home-improvement tool. It can set a mood, freshen a room, make a space feel either cozier or bigger and brighter. It can help you personalize your home and create a welcoming aura for family and friends. What other improvement is so versatile?

This book introduces you to color personalities from subtle neutrals to bold, bright hues, as well as a range of successful color combinations. We give you guidance on how and where to use color, and in what shades and proportions—all to help you make satisfying color choices. In addition, you'll find dozens of ideas for using color in your home, plus projects you can do yourself, from a painted table to wall treatments.

When you start any home-improvement project, look to our Lowe's Creative Ideas books to guide you through the process. The series includes *Makeovers, Organizing Your Home, Kids' Spaces,* and *Outdoor Living.* All can be purchased at your local Lowe's store and online at **Lowes.com**, along with books from our other series, including the recently revised edition of *Lowe's Complete Home Improvement and Repair.* They are filled with the same combination of inspiring ideas and practical information you'll find in our *Creative Ideas for Home and Garden*® magazine.

Melissa

Melissa Birdsong
Vice President, Trend, Design & Brand
Lowe's Companies, Inc.

contents

27

12

53

86

115

using color
to create
a room
you love

Color! Vibrant or subtle, patterned or plain, in large swaths or small touches, it can add new life to your home. From repainting every room in the house to adding a colorful area rug, there is no limit to the number of ways you can transform a space with color.

With page after page of exciting photos and ideas, this book aims to stimulate your imagination. We start with the most subdued shades and then work our way, chapter by chapter, to the boldest, brightest hues, showing you tones of all types and the best ways to apply them. You don't need to understand the mechanics of color to create schemes that work. But we'll show you how certain colors look better together than others, plus some tried-and-true methods to develop the most successful combinations. In this chapter you'll learn how to use color in different intensities for the best effect, how colors work together to create mood and suggest space, and which colors reinforce specific architectural styles. You'll also see how pattern, texture, and light influence your perception of color.

No matter what combinations are currently in style, selecting color for your home comes down to personal taste. You can use the examples in this book to select ones you like and note those you want to avoid. For even more ideas, turn to page 19, where you'll find suggestions on where to look for further inspiration.

Raspberry red gives this feminine bedroom a warm glow. Calming the high-energy color are dark wood tones, accessories in shades of green, and plenty of white.

The Basics of Color

Working with color is fun. While some people have an intuitive sense of how to use color to its best effect, most of us like having guidelines to help us get started. On the following pages, you'll learn five basic tips for working with color that take the mystery out of the magic. Remember, though, that rules can always be broken. The best color palette for your home is the one you love.

tip 1: color is everywhere

The first colors in any new palette are those already in residence. Take a look around you and you'll see that there is color in every item and on every surface. Notice that wood tones vary from red-browns to orange-yellows to pinkish grays. Off-white surfaces generally have a slight tone of color—a creamy yellow, a touch of green or blue, or a blush of red. Any new color you introduce to a room needs to coordinate with the colors that are already there. Consider how it will work with your existing floors, carpets, and furnishings, and whether it will complement artwork you want to highlight.

color deconstructed

Green, yellow, and a dark orange-brown are the dominant colors in this bright and cheerful kitchen. If you missed the orange at first glance, look down at the floor. It definitely contributes an important color to this punchy scheme.

Dinette set The bright yellow laminate table and vinyl chairs lay the foundation for the rest of the colors in the room. Sometimes a favorite piece of furniture inspires your color palette.

Ceiling Using a lighter shade of cream on the ceiling keeps the focus on the colorful cabinetry and backsplash.

Walls Cream-colored upper walls and white on the column and beadboard paneling provide a neutral background for the bright colors and balance their intensity.

Window trim Painting the window frames the same color as the cabinets continues the horizontal line of green across the end wall, which helps keep the ceiling from feeling too high. The geometric pattern creates an attractive focal point.

Cabinets A warm green on the cabinets is a perfect companion to the sunny yellow tile. The color gives a contemporary atmosphere to a very traditional kitchen.

Backsplash The bright yellow tile, with its shiny black accent band, was chosen to match the 1950s dinette set, a family heirloom the homeowners wanted to keep.

Hardware Chrome hardware at the sink matches the dinette table and chair frames. The glass cabinet knobs add another reflective visual treat without affecting the overall color scheme.

Floor The orange tones in the floor complement this bold palette beautifully. While wood is often considered a neutral color, it can actually vary significantly from gray to deep red to orange or yellow. If you have a lot of wood in a room, hold paint or fabric samples against it to ensure good color pairings.

tip 2: color schemes
are about relationships

All the hues you can imagine are made with a mix of three pure colors: red, blue, and yellow. When these primary colors are mixed in equal parts, they create three new ones: the secondary colors orange, green, and violet (see the color circle above). Mix pairs of these six colors and you create six more, and so on. Adding white, black, or gray can tone down any of these intense colors.

The most successful color relationships fall into one of four categories: a single-color scheme, colors next to each other in the circle, colors opposite one another, and complex schemes involving three or more colors.

▲ The familiar way to understand color relationships is to put them together in a circle, called a color wheel, with the mixed colors placed between the primaries that create them. Here, rather than show pure colors, we have arranged typical elements of home decorating—fabric, carpet, wallpaper, knobs, paint, plastic laminate—in groupings that represent the colors. You can see that each of the **six basic colors** has a kind of family of related hues—some brighter, some paler, depending on what they've been mixed with. Notice how the texture of a material affects its appearance. For example, deep blue plastic laminate appears to be brighter than deep blue pile carpet.

For a harmonious scheme, use colors that sit **next to each other** on the wheel. Here blue, green, and yellow—two primaries with the secondary that lies between them—blend compatibly. An orange scheme (think peach, which is a pale orange) can be made richer if combined with a red-orange or yellow-orange. You can accentuate certain elements in a room by assigning them the more intense values of the colors.

▶ For even more pizzazz, create a palette that combines colors: two from opposite sides of the circle, three in a triangular relationship, or four that form a rectangle. **Opposites** always catch your attention. A splash of violet can add spark to a room that is bathed in warm yellow. If you add touches of brick red and soft green, you instantly create drama in this dynamic space. In fact, such schemes may be too stimulating for some parts of the house. You may want to employ them only in playrooms or family spaces used for entertaining, such as this family room.

When a space is large and open, it can handle warm colors, like this deep brick red. Not only does this **high-energy color** make this kitchen inviting, but it has also been proven to stimulate appetite.

tip 3: color affects mood and space

Color can be used to create a desired atmosphere in a room. Particularly when deployed in large amounts—on walls, drapery, or flooring—it also has a great ability to solve problems, such as adding warmth to a room that seems chilly and helping a cramped space feel more open. You can alter mood or perceived space with color alone or by playing with the lightness and brightness of a color.

SETTING THE MOOD When you look at the traditional color wheel, you may notice that the reds, oranges, and yellows stand out as the more exciting and cheerful hues. Considered the warm colors of the spectrum, they are attention-getting. They tend to stimulate the senses, encourage activity, and create a cheerful atmosphere. Red, for instance, is a great color for a dining room because it stimulates both appetite and conversation. A soft yellow in the living room is sure to make your guests feel welcome. Muted tones of any warm color add intimacy without overpowering the space.

On the opposite side of the wheel, blues, violets, and greens make up the cool colors. These calming hues work great in bedrooms, baths, and dens where you want to encourage relaxation. Sometimes, though, cool colors can seem too cold. If you're worried about creating a chilly mood but like blues and greens, use their warmer shades, such as violet or lavender (colors that contain some red) or celadon or lime green (hues that include some yellow).

Balancing the intensity of a color scheme is another way to affect mood. For a calm space, keep the colors gentle and muted, whether they are warm or cool. For an energy-filled room, use bold, intense colors.

Any low-contrast scheme, using a single color or adjacent colors, will be calm and easy to live with. High-contrast schemes are visually exciting but may be a bit overwhelming. To keep their liveliness in check, make one hue dominant, using contrasting colors in smaller amounts.

ALTERING THE SPACE

Warm colors seem to come toward you, while cooler colors give the illusion of being farther away. By using a warm color, you can employ this effect to make a space feel cozier or to make an element of a room stand out. You might also make a room appear larger or a ceiling higher than it really is with a cool color. Similarly, painting walls a darker or more intense color, whether warm or cool, will draw the walls in for a cozy effect, while walls in a lighter or less intense color will make a space feel more open and airy. Any high-contrast scheme—say, a vibrant yellow on the walls and cobalt blue or deep lavender in drapes and upholstery—will have the same impact as a dark color, making a room feel more intimate.

Cool colors are great when you have a blemished surface or an unattractive structural element you want to hide. In a light, cool color, a flaw will fade into the background.

Color can also tie together a collection of unrelated elements. For example, upholster a sofa and a set of unmatched chairs in similar shades.

▲ A cool blue gives a small laundry room **a sense of spaciousness** and provides a relaxing atmosphere. Three related blues—on the walls, floor, and machines—create a harmonious scheme.

◀ The key to working with a cool color is to add just a hint of warmth so it does not appear too chilly or reserved. Here the bedroom maintains **a warm, relaxing atmosphere** because the greens used on the walls and ceiling have a higher percentage of yellow than blue in their makeup. The darker green headboard provides a comfortable contrast that adds interest without affecting the restful quality of the room.

tip 4: light, pattern, and texture **affect** color

The same colors can vary enormously because of light, pattern, and texture. These qualities give depth to any decor, but you'll want to be aware of their effects as you fine-tune the exact shades you choose for your home.

LIGHT   Color can go through all kinds of metamorphoses when hit by light. Furthermore, not all light is equal. During the day, the color in a corner of a room hit by natural light will look markedly different from the same color in a shady corner. At night, artificial light comes into play, and the color of that light varies. Incandescent bulbs intensify yellows and reds but dull cooler col-

ors. Some fluorescent bulbs amplify blues and greens but muddy yellows and reds. Additionally, lampshades can cast their own glows. So don't get overly attached to a paint color or fabric swatch in the store. Take it home and test it in its intended location before making a final selection.

PATTERN   Pattern enlivens a room's decor and gives color visual character. Pattern can be added to a room in many ways: through fabric, wall treatments, window coverings, floor coverings, wood grain, tile. When combining patterns, try to find things that are different enough to be interesting but similar enough to be harmonious. For instance, choose graphic shapes—stripes, squares, and circles—in a variety of sizes and colors. Or use floral motifs with common colors but a range of flower sizes.

A table lamp casts **light and shadows** across a painting, providing a rich example of how light affects color.

◄ Adding both **pattern and texture** enriches this simple green-and-white scheme. A geometric theme—striped pillows, circles in the head-board, and the grid of the quilted spread—contrasts with the rounded organic shapes on the matelassé shams. The chenille throw's soft textures balance the flat, matte surfaces in the room.

▼ A **two-toned finish** in shades of gold creates an old-world atmosphere in a small bath. You can create visual texture with different colors of paint, or add real texture with one of several new textured paint products.

The size of a pattern will affect its visual impact. Small-scale shapes tend to appear textured or solid when seen from a distance. In combination with larger patterns, they add variety. Medium-scale patterns are more versatile because they hold their shape. Large-scale patterns also hold their shape, but they make such a bold statement that you'll want to use them sparingly. Note that from a distance the eye will mix the colors in a pattern, perhaps creating a color you don't really like. So always check out patterned materials from across a room.

TEXTURE There are two types of texture: actual and visual. Actual texture is something you can feel, such as the grout lines in a tile floor or an embossed pattern in wallpaper. Actual texture modulates color in powerful ways. Its tiny peaks and valleys absorb rather than reflect light, making a color look darker and less intense. Visual texture refers to patterns that appear to the eye as texture, such as faux wood grain, the shimmery quality of a silk tapestry, or the shine of stainless steel. Visual texture creates the illusion of dimension. Smooth, shiny surfaces, because they have no real texture, reflect light and can make a color both lighter and brighter. When working with a simple color scheme, you can give it more excitement by combining several kinds of texture. A more complex scheme can be balanced with a single kind of texture.

tip 5: architecture can guide color decisions

The architectural style of your home—or the style you'd like to suggest—provides plenty of inspiration for color selection. Many historical periods had distinctive palettes. If you have an authentic period house, ask at Lowe's for the American Tradition National Trust line of paints, more than 250 colors that reflect historic homes such as The Homestead in Virginia. You may find the guidelines here helpful. Remember, though, the best guideline is to go with what works for the way you live.

◄ Traditional architecture is formal, including styles such as **Georgian and Victorian.** With their more ornate detailing, they can handle a certain richness of color. Darker shades—such as deep reds, purples, blues, and greens—make great choices for walls and upholstery. In lighter hues, cream, pea green, deep pink, salmon, mauve, blue-green, and lilac are historically appropriate. If your taste leans toward less color, warm beiges, browns, and light terra-cottas can add sophistication to a traditional home. Pattern and texture can be more elaborate in these houses. In this room, a striped drapery ties together the gilded mirror frame and the rich red of the walls, while white paint on the trim keeps the color from being overwhelming.

▼ **Contemporary design** ranges from steel-and-glass modern to ranch styles. Its variety and clean lines mean almost anything goes in terms of color schemes, from all white to different colors in every room. Typically, contemporary designs feature solid colors and geometrics rather than patterns and florals. Here green, blue, white, and stainless steel gray combine with rectangular forms for a clean look.

Simplicity is the key to **casual style,** which includes Colonial, Arts and Crafts, Cottage, and Southwest. Earth tones such as ochre, almond, rust, brown, sage green, and both green- and blue-grays work well in such homes. Walls may be left white, or pastels like pale yellows, blues, and pinks may be paired with white wood. Also consider stencils or wallpaper borders on walls as colorful decorative elements. Here the border of trees—a natural motif typical of Arts and Crafts design—just below the ceiling not only adds whimsy but moves the eye up the wall to create a sense of greater height.

Getting Started

Whether you want to add a little zip to a room that has the blahs or you plan to strip a room down to its bare walls and floor joists and start from scratch, the first step is to define the function of the space and the atmosphere you want to create. Then note all the colors that remain in the room, since they are the first shades in your new palette. With that accomplished, you're ready to start playing with color.

how much color?

It's important to ask yourself how much color you want. When you walk into a bright red room, do you feel overjoyed or overwhelmed? Are soft pastels soothing on your psyche or too delicate? Is the sophistication of a white or neutral background just the answer for your collection of colorful artwork and accessories? And how many different colors do you want

▶ Your garden can **inspire** an effective color scheme. Select the colors you love best, considering both foliage and blossoms.

▼ A **two-color scheme** unites this living room, dining room, and the hall between. The red from the living room rug covers the walls of the dining room, while the rug's gold tones appear on the other walls. Both colors are picked up in the plaid fabric on pillows and dining chairs.

in any given room—a single color in a few shades or a jazzy set of multiple colors? To test yourself, you can experiment with color. Try repainting walls and ceilings; changing slipcovers, throws, and bed and bath linens; or moving colorful accessories from one room to another.

If you're redoing your entire home, consider carrying the same color or set of colors from room to room to create a smooth visual transition. By using different colors in every room, you create distinctly separate spaces, which can be effective in a large home but may feel uncoordinated in a small one. Whenever you use lots of colors, keep them similar in tone. The rooms will look different yet unified.

finding inspiration

There are many excellent sources for color ideas, starting with this book, which is organized by types of color, from the very subtlest neutrals to the boldest brights. Not only do we suggest hundreds of ways to combine and apply colors, but we also include lots of how-to projects that enable you to create some great looks in your own home.

▲ Borrow a color palette from favorite **accessories,** such as this set of glass vases. Such bright colors can be dominant or may be used as accents in a room with very little color.

In addition, you can look around your environment for a wealth of ideas to guide you. A garden bed, a scrap of colorful wallpaper, a favorite flower, a rug, a china pattern, or a piece of upholstery fabric may provide inspiration for a winning combination of colors. You can also borrow a palette from a favorite painting or even a restaurant you like. Collect every possibility that strikes your fancy and then decide which colors are the most appealing and effective for your home.

Sometimes too many color choices may be a bit overwhelming. Lowe's can help you narrow your options. See page 21 for a review of our color-selection services.

a color
primer

Ultimately, your color decisions will be based on personal preference. However, you may want to back up your choices with a more detailed understanding. This chapter offers the meat and bones of working with color: basic terminology, with examples of how the color wheel can help you create a scheme; using color as a problem solver; coordinating colors from one room to the next; and how to use accents most effectively.

Your nearby Lowe's store can provide paint-selection help in a number of ways. In our store displays you'll find dozens of photos and cards showing a wide range of beautifully coordinated color palettes to suit individual preferences and different moods. Lowe's paint department features a free computerized color matching system. Bring in anything from a ceramic plate to a fabric swatch and our paint professionals will match it for you. Our Virtual Painter software will instantly colorize any of more than 40 designer room scenes. Import digital photos of the rooms you will be painting and test colors. You can find the software online at **Lowes.com** by selecting "Interactive Design Tools" under the Project Center heading. You can also purchase it online or at your nearby Lowe's store. Or go online to **Lowes.com/Paint**. You'll find a range of how-to information and buying guides, as well as "fan decks" of paint colors you can purchase, to help ensure the success of any painting project.

When you are comfortable with the knowledge of how color works, you can use any of your favorite hues to create a room you love. Here an unorthodox combination of **pink, yellow, orange, and blue** works because the colors are of equal strength.

The Color Wheel

The color wheel helps you see how to put various combinations together effectively. The 12 basic colors fall into three categories: primary (red, blue, yellow), secondary (green, violet, orange), and intermediate (yellow-orange and other hybrids).

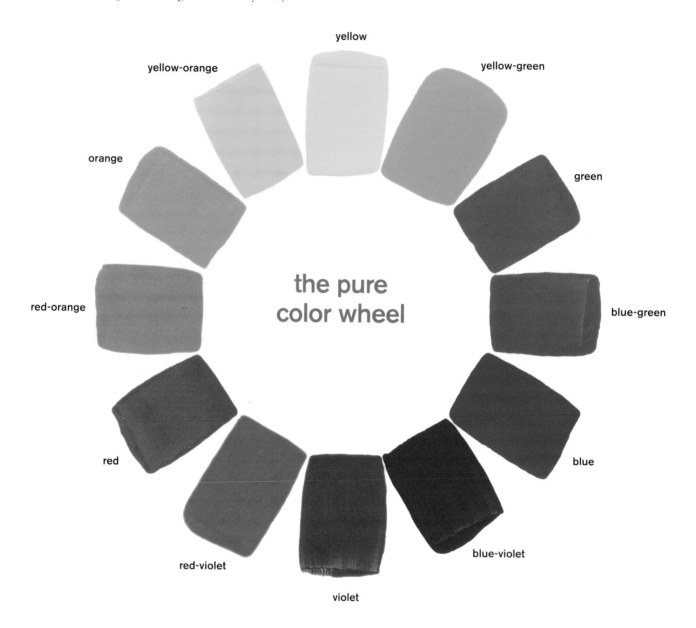

yellow

yellow-orange

yellow-green

orange

green

red-orange

blue-green

the pure
color wheel

red

blue

red-violet

blue-violet

violet

The wheel here shows the pure colors in their full **intensity**. Intensity measures purity or brightness. Pure, high-intensity colors are easy to spot because of their brilliance (think of fire engine red or cobalt blue). The pure colors can be lightened or darkened with the addition of white, black, or gray, creating different **values**. It's easy to confuse intensity and value, but they are not the same. When you look at a color, first ask yourself, "Is it light, medium, or dark?" That's the value. Then ask, "Is it bright or dull?" That's the intensity.

For most decorating schemes, pure colors are too powerful. Low-intensity colors like those illustrated at right are usually more successful.

light-value,
low-intensity colors

medium-value,
low-intensity colors

medium-light-value,
low-intensity colors

dark-value,
low-intensity colors

Color Schemes

Chapter One introduces color combinations in general terms. Here, for a bit more detail, you'll find the terms used by professional designers.

Successful color combinations fall into four basic categories, ranging from very subtle to extremely dynamic. In general, the most harmonious designs use colors in unequal quantities, with one dominant color and one or more supporting ones. However, you can use colors in equal quantities if their values and intensities are similar (see page 29 for examples).

monochromatic schemes

These designs involve a single color used in one or more values and intensities. You can add interest to a monochromatic scheme with a little black, white, or gray.

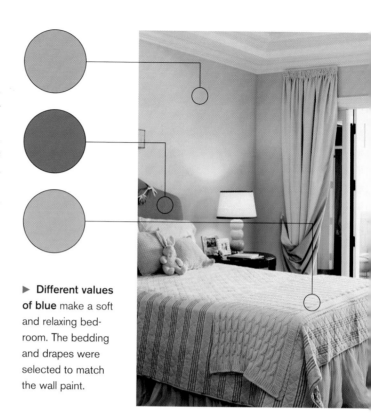

▶ **Different values of blue** make a soft and relaxing bedroom. The bedding and drapes were selected to match the wall paint.

analogous schemes

Using hues that lie next to each other on the color wheel—for example, red and red-orange or blue-green and green—analogous schemes are held together by the common color (red in the first example and green in the second). To avoid monotony, vary the quantities and intensities of the colors and mix in some lively patterns and textures.

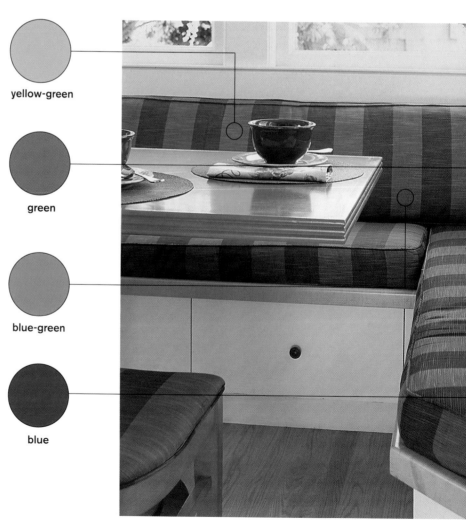

yellow-green

green

blue-green

blue

▶ **Blue, blue-green, and yellow-green** striped cushions blend handsomely with the green walls behind them. The analogous scheme is continued on the tabletop, with blue bowls on green placemats.

complementary schemes

These two-color schemes are based on a pair of colors that lie directly across from each other on the wheel. Green and red are complements, as are blue and orange. In a room, two complementary colors will visually intensify each other. For example, a pale violet sofa in front of a yellow wall will make the yellow shine. Using intermediate colors, such as turquoise and terra-cotta or brick red and juniper green, or using quieter values, will temper such a high-contrast scheme. The scheme is still effective if the complements are not quite opposite—for instance, a yellow-green with violet.

▲ The orange tone of the wood vanity is the **complement to the blue** mosaic tile. With white accents, they make for a light and airy bath.

orange   blue

yellow

red

blue

complex schemes

A combination of several colors that are neither complementary nor analogous is a complex scheme. Well chosen, such schemes are pleasing because they automatically balance the visual temperature, using both cool and warm colors.

Three-color combinations generally pull together hues that are spaced evenly around the wheel. Think of a sage green wall with accents of salmon and pink. Another approach is to select a single color and add the colors that flank its complement. For instance, combine blue with the two colors that flank orange: red-orange and yellow-orange. This is called a split-complement three-color combination.

A four-color scheme could include colors that are equidistant on the color wheel, or two complementary pairs of colors that are separated from each other by only one position on the wheel. Salmon and yellow, for example, create a dynamic scheme when paired with blue and violet.

▲ This **three-color** scheme features the primaries—red, blue, and yellow—which are equidistant on the wheel. Additional colors— a strip of pink tile, the orange-toned cabinets—soften the contrast in this vibrant bath.

► Four pastel stripes—pink, green, yellow-orange, and blue-violet—work beautifully together because the colors are **equidistant on the color wheel**. Deeper shades of these colors appear in the bedding and accessories around the room.

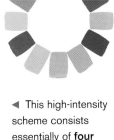

red

orange

blue

green

◄ This high-intensity scheme consists essentially of **four colors**: complementary red and green paired with complementary blue and orange.

pink

green

yellow-orange

blue-violet

Color as a Problem Solver

Color, particularly paint, is one of the most economical ways to solve spatial and visual problems without ripping out walls or rebuilding. Cool colors—blue, green, and violet—and light colors visually recede, so use them to make a room feel larger or taller or to hide unattractive elements. Darker colors, especially the warm tones, seem to advance, so use shades of red, orange, and yellow when you want a space to envelop you or an object to stand out.

▶ In a tiny bedroom, a **slate blue ceiling** with fairy lights seems sky high, taking the focus off the small size of the room.

the details
improving accessibility with color

Color can be used effectively to provide visual cues for people with limited vision. Here a contrasting color strip highlights the shape and location of the counter edge. Tops of stairways or single steps that separate a room into two levels can also be a hazard for people with poor eyesight. Consider painting or inlaying a contrasting color strip on the top step to call attention to the elevation change.

color from room to room

Every room can have its own personality and set of colors when you consider the whole house as a single color scheme rather than several individual ones. Use the same color trim throughout the house to tie the rooms together (white is always effective).

▲ Use the secondary and intermediate colors to link color schemes in primary hues. Here a green palm creates a **color transition** between the bright blue and yellow walls of adjoining rooms.

▶ Echoed in the tulips on the table, deep tones of yellow, red, and green keep the eye moving from the hallway to the dining room to the back of the built-in hutch. Because the colors are of **similar intensity,** they coexist well.

If you can't hide it, flaunt it! **Add pizzazz** to your kitchen with smaller elements such as a red teakettle and toaster and a bright yellow mixer. Appliances and cookware are now available in a range of bright hues to complement today's most popular color schemes.

Details That Make a Difference

The trick to using color accents effectively is to coordinate them with your overall scheme, providing enough contrast to make them stand out: a purple teakettle in an all-yellow kitchen, a bright red telephone in a neutral-toned home office, an aqua vase in a red and orange living room. The most attractive spaces are thought out down to the last detail.

► Even small touches can carry a color from one part of a room to another. Bright baskets and **basket liners** have the additional benefit of being practical.

▼ Risers in soft shades of blue and violet add personality to this simple staircase. Decorative elements such as ceramic tiles, wood inlays, and stencils can add color to any important **architectural feature.**

subtle neutrals

n

Neutral color schemes are tranquil and soothing, and they work well in most homes. Such designs are simple and understated, yet they can be totally in tune with today's trends, given the right combination of tones and textures. Neutral walls make an excellent backdrop for striking furniture and art. And these quiet colors are great for faux finishes, showing off complex texture and pattern when hit by light. If a neutral scheme seems a tad subdued for your taste, brightly colored accessories and artwork can add zing.

With neutrals, you have a much larger palette than you might imagine, starting with the true neutrals—white, black, and gray—which are considered "noncolors." Mix in the popular shades of tan, beige, and brown and you have a few more options that never go out of style. In addition to those basics, neutrals today include hues that are actually very subtle versions of color: pale celadon, beiges that lean slightly toward blue or pink, off-whites with just a slight amount of color. These soft shades lend ambience and a hint of color to a room but never overwhelm or stand out.

In this chapter we'll show you a range of rooms decorated in neutrals, from white, black, and gray to these neutralized colors. You'll see how you can use neutrals everywhere—on walls, floors, and furnishings—without fear of overdoing it, as well as ideas for adding contrast, pattern, and texture to any neutral scheme.

A neutral color scheme creates a soothing atmosphere for an elegant master bath retreat. An assortment of textures adds vitality to this **soft combination** of colors.

Shades of Difference

A brief review of true neutrals and neutralized colors will help you work with these popular shades.

true neutrals

Black, white, and gray are classics, always in style. As noncolors, these true neutrals hold their own in any scheme without adding color or altering existing color relationships. Whether used alone or together, they can be extremely sophisticated, but they can also seem stark. To be sure a true neutral scheme is inviting, you can use colorful accents. Also consider the impact of texture. Enliven a black-and-white scheme with black velvet draperies or a leather sofa, or add shiny gray metal hardware to your cabinetry. Texture creates visual interest, and the effect of light and shadow will enhance each hue.

WHITE White is well known for creating a bright and airy look because it reflects light. It's also a great design problem solver. Use white in rooms with irregular features; in the absence of color, minor flaws will nearly disappear. Paint doors, mouldings, and trim white to break up expanses of color and emphasize the lines of a room. White furnishings and draperies are great because they fit in anywhere.

If you decide to go with a white theme, be aware that very few whites are pure. In fact, a true white, devoid of all color, is rarely used on walls because it is too cold and stark. Most white paints contain undertones of warm or cool colors. Compare a number of possibilities to select the white that works for you.

BLACK While there are teenagers who might convince you that an all-black scheme is pretty cool, black is most often used as an accent. Wrought iron bed frames, tile trim, countertops, and leather sofas are just a few examples of how you can incorporate black into your home decor. Graphic and sophisticated, black works best in small doses.

▶ The sophisticated use of **black and white** tiles and a white tub surround pairs modern luxury with the classic elegance of 1920s style. The glass block, which matches the neutral blue-gray wall, adds just enough texture to soften the look.

◀ An **all-white** scheme opens up a cottage bath by reflecting light. A black step and picture frame and a gray chrome faucet add depth and visual interest.

GRAY The all-purpose neutral gray became highly fashionable in the 1930s era of Art Deco and continues to be a good match with any modern decor. A mixture of black and white, gray bridges the gaps between other colors without taking over. Gray can be introduced through slate or marble flooring, through upholstery fabric, or in metallic tones, such as nickel-finish door pulls, stainless steel appliances, or a silver tea service.

▼ This **all-gray** bath succeeds through the use of pattern and texture. The combination of rectangular marble tiles around the tub and small hexagonal ones on the floor gives life to the neutral color, while the shiny chrome fixtures add a bit of sparkle to this quiet scheme.

A garage remodel is **brightened** by white on the cabinetry and peg-board; dark laminate countertops make a practical work surface. The neutral color scheme gains shine from the faux stainless steel finish on the peg-board.

what a great idea

stylish hangups

For a large impact in a small space, hang several white shelves in different sizes against a neutral wall. Adorn them with black-framed photos or shadow boxes. This attractive design element comes in a variety of styles, from traditional carved mantelshelves to square-edged, modern, bracketless ones. The shelves can be lined up horizontally, stacked vertically, or offset in a zigzag pattern.

neutralized color

You can create neutral colors by adding white or black to any color to lower its intensity, or you can mix a touch of one color to a larger amount of its complement. For example, a little green added to red creates a neutral red, and a little red added to green creates a neutral green. When you are combining different neutrals, it helps to identify the source color for each one, such as red, blue, or yellow. The simplest way to work with these colors is to use various shades from the same family—a mix of soft, neutral greens, for instance. But you can also combine neutrals in the same way you'd work with bolder colors, by mixing complements or colors that sit together on the color wheel (see pages 22–27).

▶ The **subtlety** of the warm yellow-green makes this wall color a neutral rather than a pastel. It provides an elegant backdrop for the black-and-tan vanities as well as the rich tones of the floor.

An inviting home office gets its interest from **minor changes** in the beige and brown tones, as well as a variety of actual and visual textures.

▲ A variety of neutrals balances the warm tones of cherry cabinetry in this kitchen. **Rich texture** is everywhere, from the tile backsplash, vinyl floor, and granite countertops to the stainless steel appliances and glass-fronted cabinet doors.

◀ A two-toned beige paint scheme adds depth and richness to this comfortable sitting room. The **neutral browns** and deep reds in the throw pillows provide understated pattern and texture without compromising the restful atmosphere these colors create.

► A **neutral green** color scheme is both elegant and easy to work with. It can also provide a subtle backdrop for colorful art and accessories.

▼ Here the cherry cabinetry, cream-colored walls, and warm brown quartz countertops combine different tones of **neutral yellow** and brown. Black appliances and accessories blend into the scheme without dominating it.

decorating

artful display

Artwork and neutral color schemes are natural partners. The art adds color to the low-key design, while neutral tones on the wall cause the painting to pop out. You can also use an accent color, drawn from the artwork, on the wall.

Creative lighting is critical for showcasing art. Recessed lights offer overall illumination while spotlighting a piece of art from above. Angled cable lighting is perfect for displaying art in a long hallway or on a large wall. Small picture lights can illuminate individual pieces.

home gallery tips

- Treat each piece with care. Never place art in direct sunlight, as ultraviolet rays can cause damage.
- Hang artwork at eye level for the person of average height. However, in a room where people generally are seated (such as a dining room), hang pieces slightly lower.
- When separate works are grouped, spacing is important. Either too close together or too far apart will look odd. Consider spaces of 2½ to 3 inches as a general guideline.

▲ The picture light, plugged into a baseboard receptacle, gives this painting the **spotlight** it deserves.

▶ A section of one wall in a white room is painted a vibrant, warm orange, ensuring that the painting is the major **focal point** in the room.

▼ In a niche, the neutral wall color gives way to an **accent panel** of bright orange. Bathed by recessed lighting, the painting glows in this dramatic setting.

Pairing Neutrals with Architectural Styles

Neutrals are particularly suited to modern design, which is characterized by white or wood-paneled walls and natural finishes. White always enhances a cottage-style home, and light stone colors are typically used in Mediterranean architecture. But a neutral palette complements virtually any architectural style. Even in styles that celebrate color, such as Southwest or Victorian, you can use neutralized shades of period colors to honor the design.

▼ A pale green glaze color-washed over the walls gives an old-world feel to this **casual** living room. Various tones of beige, brown, and green in the furnishings and accessories—including the rough wood beams—coexist harmoniously because of the integrating effect of this soft neutral background. A painting over the fireplace and a vase of cut flowers provide all the color this room needs.

◄ Sleek and seamless are hallmarks of **contemporary** design, and the natural, neutral colors in this kitchen punctuate those qualities. The high contrast between light surfaces—walls, ceiling, and floor—and dark countertops and appliances creates a sophistication typical of modern design.

► The **traditional** style of the furniture and the deep mouldings of this room are set off by cream walls and white trim. White upholstery and a neutral-toned area rug complete the scheme. It's appropriate for the somewhat formal style, and at the same time it allows the colorful accessories to stand out.

Color Schemes That Work

Though neutral interiors often look effortlessly natural, they need as much attention as any other color scheme. If you have the luxury of remodeling a space from scratch, you can pick your floor, ceiling, and wall colors first and then add furnishings and accessories to complement their colors. If you have existing furnishings, consider their dominant hues and add neutrals that mix well with them.

▼ Light and dark neutrals contrast to create a soothing bath retreat. A red-hued wood-slat step serves as a transition between the dark wood walls and light limestone tub surround, showing how you can **soften a stark contrast** with a medium-toned neutral.

▶ This master bedroom demonstrates how you can create a sophisticated and relaxing retreat with minimal color. Shades of **beige, brown, and neutral green** work beautifully together here. Pattern in the linens and artwork, along with texture on the shades, rug, and glossy bed frame, introduces variety.

Brown and gray make a beautiful pair in this spacious kitchen. Visual texture is the key to the success of this scheme, as the glossy surface of the cabinets contrasts with the grid of the tile backsplash and the speckled texture of the solid-surface countertop on the island. Note how the gray countertop is edged with a band of brown. An antique-white island base and black appliances add interest without affecting the color scheme.

▲ Urban chic was the goal of the **fashionable color palette** for this hospitality center. Pewter-glazed cabinetry with the slightest touch of red sets a warm and inviting atmosphere. An off-white solid-surface countertop balances the darker finish of the cabinets and breaks up the space horizontally to give this corner a more spacious feel. The slightly darker off-white porcelain floor tiles pick up the pewter undertones of the cabinets, visually anchoring the room without drawing the eye downward. With this rich neutral scheme, it takes only a single element of strong color—a complementary green plate— to add spark.

The wallpaper in these charming alcoves is true to Victorian decor, which is known for its **patterns.** The subtle rose design contributes a welcome touch of color.

Base coat: American Tradition, Savannah Red #1008-7B, eggshell
Glaze color: American Tradition, Churchill Hotel Brown #3010-9

American Tradition, Homestead Resort Cream #7002-23

American Tradition, Damask Dunes #1006-10B

◄ From the lightest beige to the darkest russet brown, this bath is washed in **warm neutrals.** Victorian-inspired elements combine with period colors to provide a touch of nostalgia in a modern retreat. The homeowners used limestone-like ceramic tiles for the floor and tub surround as the starting point for this warm color palette. The wall color matches the darker ivory tones of the tile, while the lacy curtains and wallpaper pick up its lighter shades. The bright white of the old-fashioned claw-foot tub establishes this period piece as the room's major focal point. The rose and red touches of the bronze hardware, floral urns, wooden pedestal table, and claret-colored glazed ceiling create an attractive contrast to the lighter neutrals in the room.

◄ The **high contrast** between light vanilla and coffee-brown cabinets lends a farmhouse feel to this large and open kitchen. The copper and light brown tones of the granite countertop, stone backsplash tiles, and wood floor soften the contrast.

glossing it over

A great way to add color to a room, glazing can transform a bare wall or ceiling into an interesting focal point. And with tintable translucent glaze, you can have a custom color to suit your palette.

For a finishing touch to their remodeled bath, the owners of this house glazed their newly installed ceiling tiles. Glazing works best on a textured surface like this; you can also try it on paintable embossed wallpaper.

Step 1: After installing the ceiling tiles, apply painter's tape to the top of the wall. Roll the tiles with basecoat. Let it dry, and repeat if necessary.

Step 2: Follow the directions on the label to tint the glaze with the glaze color.

Step 3: Working in one 3-foot-square section at a time, apply the tintable glaze to the tiles with a brush. Gently rub off the glaze with a damp sheet of rag-rolling cotton until you achieve the desired effect. Repeat until the entire ceiling is covered.

Lowe's list

materials
- tiles (Armstrong, Tin Look, Model 1240, special order)
- drop cloth
- painter's tape
- roller kit
- paintbrush
- rag-rolling cotton

paint
- basecoat (American Tradition, Savannah Red #1008-7B, eggshell)
- glaze (American Tradition, Interior Translucent Tintable Glaze #34128)
- glaze color (American Tradition, Churchill Hotel Brown #3010-9)

Skill level: Beginner

Rough cost estimate: $95*

Rough time estimate: 1 day** (depending on room size)

*Does not include labor costs or applicable taxes, which may vary by market, or the cost of the ceiling tiles.
**Does not include lead time for special-order materials.

how much paint?

When purchasing paint, take your room's measurements to Lowe's and check can labels for coverage guidelines. Typically, a gallon of paint covers 300 to 400 square feet of smooth surface. If your ceiling or walls have a rough texture, are unfinished, or require more than one coat, you'll need more paint for proper coverage.

◄ Tiling the shower surround and bathtub in shades of **neutral green** greatly enriches a simple black-and-white scheme. The tiny squares of the glass mosaic tile coordinate well with the other rectangular shapes in the room.

◄ Subtle variations of beige and soft yellow neutrals result in a comfortable but opulent living room. All of the room's hues unite in the patterned rug.

The ceiling, sometimes called the "fifth wall," offers an opportunity to add style to a room. **Embossed ceiling tiles,** along with horizontal blinds and a soft fabric curtain on the door, keep this taupe-and-white room from feeling too severe.

Texture and Pattern in a Neutral Scheme

Texture and pattern always matter when it comes to home decorating. But the more color-free a scheme, the more it depends on these elements for visual interest. The texture and pattern of wood wainscot or wooden window blinds can enliven an all-white room. A gray textured rug will soften a black floor. The shine of antique gold frames adds vitality to beige walls. Consider a generous mix of materials when you accessorize a neutral scheme. And if the look remains too austere, don't be afraid to add a touch of color. (See pages 122–125 for ideas.)

pulling it together

Once you've determined what neutrals you want to work with, look for ways to add texture or pattern to several of the surfaces in the room. The examples on these pages show how just the right amount of each makes a neutral scheme livelier.

▶ The inspiration for this bath remodel, with its creamy marble surfaces and weathered plaster walls of yellow-gold, came from the Tuscany region of Italy. The homeowners wanted to add the **texture** of these materials to their neutral color scheme. For the bath surround, they chose ceramic tile with the appearance of tumbled marble. The acanthus-leaf border tile lends a three-dimensional touch. For the walls, a faux finish of Venetian plaster and paint mimics the look of weathered plaster.

To learn more about how to work with Venetian plaster, visit **Lowes.com**, search with the phrase "Venetian plaster," and click on "Venetian Plaster Finish" under Project Center.

◀ Black, white, and tan always make for an appealing scheme in a modern kitchen. But this room might look flat were it not for the spots of metal gleaming throughout: the collection of chrome toasters on display, the door and drawer pulls, the wall clock, the stainless steel countertop and appliances. The **geometric patterns** formed by grout lines in the black slate floor and tile backsplash, and even by the cabinet edges, break up the expanses of flat color.

▶ This sitting area is surprisingly lively, considering its limited palette of neutral beige, gold, and brown. Vitality glows from the **pattern and sheen** in the striped chair fabric, the warmth of the colors, the nubbly texture of the sisal rug underfoot, and the shine of the polished silver table lamp.

behind the design

it's hip to be square

A subtle color scheme and a geometric motif on the walls and floor lend a contemporary, Zen-like feel to this remodeled bath suite. The bold squares and rich neutral hues of the moisture-resistant wallpaper add minimalist style. Dark-stained moulding complements the console and mirror trim, while the color of the door and casing echoes the neutral green in the wallpaper.

The room is a study in comfortable contrasts. Just as dark contrasts with light, the round shapes of the sinks and lamp-shades play well against the squares and rectangles on the walls, floor, mirrors, and vanities. The shiny glass vanity tops reflect light and stand out against the matte finish of the walls and floor.

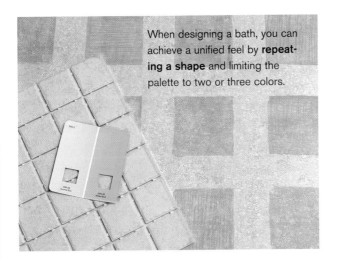

When designing a bath, you can achieve a unified feel by **repeating a shape** and limiting the palette to two or three colors.

accessorizing

Often you can provide a scheme with all the pattern and texture it needs by adding a few well-chosen accessories. Furniture and rugs are obvious choices, but sometimes a single sculpture or piece of artwork can do the trick. If you have a neutral scheme that looks a little flat, introduce accessories one by one until you achieve the right effect.

WINDOW COVERING Don't overlook the window as an opportunity for adding to a neutral room. Horizontal blinds give a clean, graphic pattern to the wall, as well as great privacy and light control. Wooden blinds with 2- or 3-inch slats have a look similar to that of plantation shutters at a lower price. In addition, decorative tape on the blinds can coordinate with other elements in the room.

FLOOR COVERING With innovative—and affordable—carpet tiles, the possibilities for creating pattern on your floors are endless. You can carpet an average-size room or create an area rug in an afternoon. Simply arrange the easy-to-install blocks of color using peel-off adhesive dots instead of glue or tacks. Individual tiles can be replaced as necessary. The tiles come in a range of colors in addition to these neutral tones.

FABRIC A length of patterned fabric can jazz up any room, whether it is functional, like this shower curtain, or just decorative. Here the homeowner has selected a striped canvas to highlight the walls' warm tone. She mounted it from the ceiling and let it fall to the floor. The length of the fabric coupled with the vertical stripes draws the eye up, visually enlarging the space.

HARDWARE Hardware with interesting textures, finishes, and shapes will stand out boldly in a neutral scheme, and it may be the only accessory you need. These stainless steel pulls with their perforated texture and curved shape balance straight lines in a contemporary kitchen.

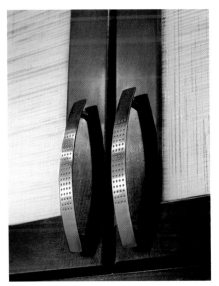

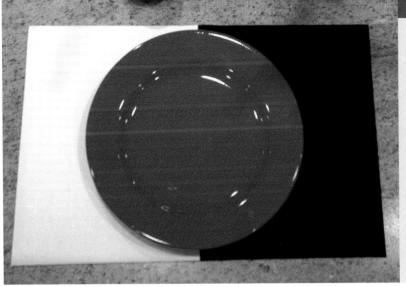

what a great idea

geometric place mats

Black and white can be used against any neutral color without changing the color relationships. Using a utility knife, cut a 9- × 12-inch rectangle from black vinyl drawer-liner material. Cut a same-size rectangle from white vinyl liner. (Liner can be found in Lowe's home organization department.) Align a 12-inch edge of the black rectangle with a corresponding edge of the white one to create a 12- × 18-inch mat. Use duct tape across the back seam of the two panels to attach them; trim any excess tape. You can make a total of eight place mats with one roll of black and one roll of white vinyl liner.

soft pastels

Pastels may be the most versatile shades of the color world. Used alone, they are gentle and soothing, creating a soft elegance that is both romantic and inviting. In combination with other colors, both pastel and more vibrant, they can make a lively contribution, adding balance to the overall design.

This chapter introduces you to the world of pastels and the variety of ways they can add character to your home. These hues are so adaptable that they can be used freely in decorating without being overwhelming. Pastel walls can pick up on the colors of a room's accessories or architectural features without competing with them. They can also energize a room full of neutral furniture. If you're a fan of neutral walls, think about adding pastel shades to wood trim and ceilings for a subtle but interesting effect. For example, in a white room, try celadon green on wainscot or doors, or a soft blue on a bedroom ceiling. Or dress up a neutral background by covering your sofas, chairs, or windows with floral-patterned fabrics in these satisfying hues.

A view of Washington's Mount Rainier inspired the color scheme in this Northwestern home. The colors of the **forest, earth, sky, and lake** appear in the soft pastels, which subtly merge with one another to create an atmosphere of tranquility. The rug, lamps, and throw pillows add deeper and brighter blues and greens to make the whole room come alive.

More Than Pink and Baby Blue

The word *pastel* tends to conjure images of sweet nurseries, but there's more to these shades than that. A pastel is any color significantly lightened by white, including peach, lavender, pale aqua, and soft coral.

Pastels play well together. Because of their lightness, there's little concern about clashing. Use several together in one room, or use a different color in each adjoining room.

Any pastel will make a room seem larger, creating an open and airy atmosphere. These are wonderful colors in rooms that get a lot of use, such as kitchens and baths, because they are so cheerful and easy on the eye. Likewise, they are a good choice in bedrooms because of their relaxing effect. Pastels can also brighten a room that contains a lot of dark furniture, such as a dining room, making it feel less formal and serious.

Pale versions of cool colors—baby blue and light green, for instance—work best in areas where you want to instill calm. Light shades of any of the warm colors—such as pink, salmon, yellow, red-violet, and even lime green—will add freshness and vitality to living rooms, dining rooms, and kitchens, whether or not you embolden the scheme with brighter colors. Feminine pinks will always add a dash of romance to your decor.

▲ A young girl's room is the perfect location for a **luscious mixture** of pastels. Yellow, green, blue, and pink make a fresh combination that this child can enjoy for many years.

▶ Basking in natural light, a child's bath glows from the **soft shades** of yellow in the tiles.

American Tradition, Pirate's Treasure #3006-5B

American Tradition, Organic Garden #6005-6B

Just because pastels are pale does not mean they are bland. In this contemporary bath, a **crisp teal**-and-white scheme evokes the serenity of a spa.

Pairing Pastels with Architectural Styles

Pastels are especially appropriate in traditional styles, where they create a quiet back-drop for elegant living. In casual homes, their soft tones can contribute to an informal feel. For a contemporary look, pair a pastel with white. Soft periwinkle blue walls and white subway tiles, for example, are a great combination for a modern bath. If you use soft colors in period homes that would typically boast bolder color, use faded hues of the period palette, such as a pale olive green in an Arts and Crafts home or a light mauve in a Victorian one.

▼ In this **contemporary** living room, pastel yellow lightens the tone set by the dark furnishings.

A soft olive green wall serves as a natural-toned backdrop for white-painted wood in a **casual** entryway.

▶ Pastel blue upholstery and accents create a fresh atmosphere in this **traditional** living room. Touches of pink in the throw pillows and rug warm the cool color.

Color Schemes That Work

The most restful pastel schemes use a single color in one or more shades, or two colors that blend, such as aqua and teal, pale lime green and yellow, or lavender and pink. For more vibrancy, choose colors that contrast, such as salmon and light blue, or mint green and rose. When working with a multicolor pastel design, you'll find that the look is most pleasing if all the colors have a similar tone, as in the living room pictured on pages 70–71.

schemes that blend

At its best, a simple pastel palette creates a sense of comfort that is friendly and inviting. It introduces modest color that doesn't compete with other design features in a room, making it a good choice when you want to let artwork, furniture, or some special accessory take center stage. Add depth to a simple plan by using several pastels of the same color, such as a pale yellow as background for a wall or sofa and a slightly deeper yellow for trim. When you select more than one color, create harmony by using similar tones. On the next few pages, you'll see schemes featuring single pastels or closely related ones, as well as a few fun projects you can do yourself to add color to any room.

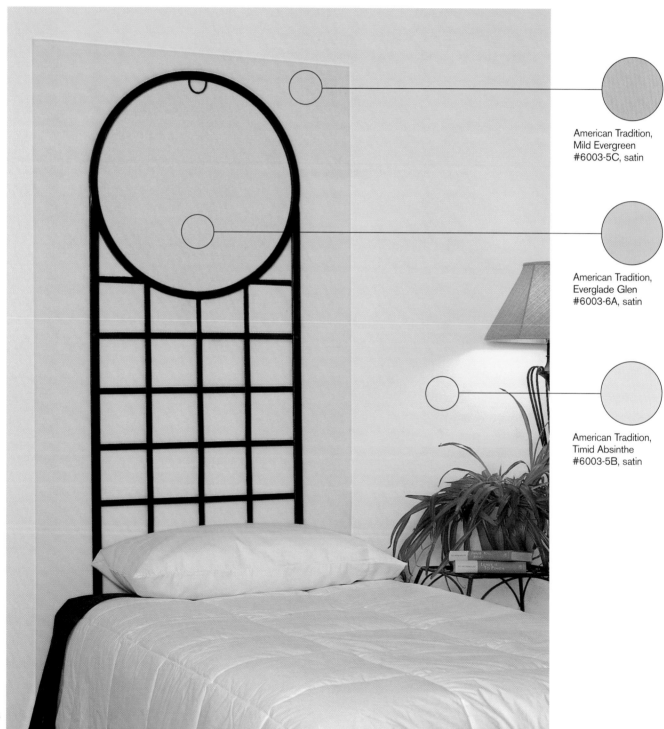

American Tradition, Mild Evergreen #6003-5C, satin

American Tradition, Everglade Glen #6003-6A, satin

American Tradition, Timid Absinthe #6003-5B, satin

Pastel pink is still the most popular color for a young girl's bedroom. Here the **three shades of pink** were inspired by some of the child's favorite things: dress-up clothes, dancewear, roses, and bubble gum. The dominant hue is a soft pink, but darker and lighter shades cleverly break the monotony.

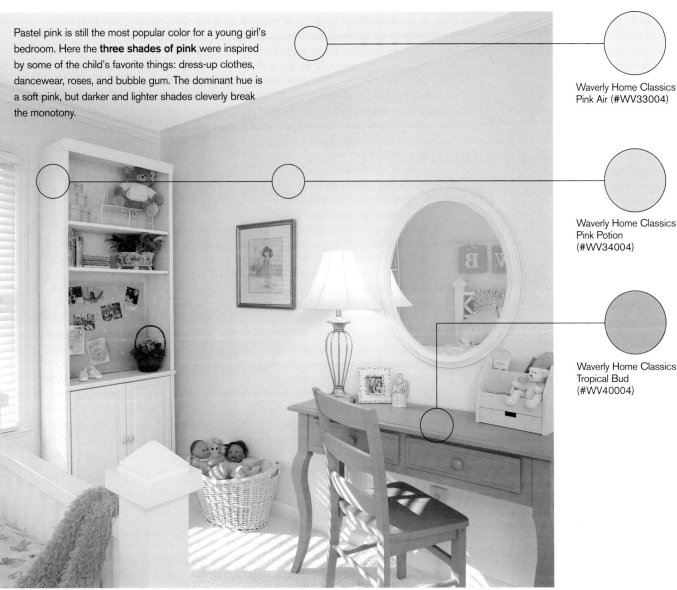

Waverly Home Classics
Pink Air (#WV33004)

Waverly Home Classics
Pink Potion
(#WV34004)

Waverly Home Classics
Tropical Bud
(#WV40004)

◀ Three shades of pastel green combine to create an **open airiness** in this simple bedroom. The walls are painted in the lightest shade of green. A panel behind the bed is one shade darker, and the inside of the circle is darker still. A black window trellis attached to the wall serves as a headboard.

quick and easy project

light up a lamp

Customize a lampshade to add a pretty pastel beside the bed. Shown atop a medium white base, this 14-inch shade has a simple design created with latex paint. Get creative, practice on poster board, and have fun showing off your personality.

▲ A fresh, **light sage green** is so versatile that it was used on all the walls throughout this home. Fabric and accessories provide additional color.

◄ A dash of pastel transforms a stark white bath with a touch of glamour. **Green glass tile** used sparingly as a decorative accent was an affordable luxury for the budget-minded owners of this home.

This guestroom serves as a retreat where overnight visitors can relax. Two **shades of lavender** for the walls and ceiling produce a calming effect. Painting the side table a shade darker than the wall and decorating the bed with a matching lavender spread maintain the mood. The headboard, painted a coffee color, stands out against the wall as a focal point. Since lavender and coffee brown both contain red, these colors mix well together. For how-to instructions on creating the headboard, log on to **LowesCreativeIdeas.com** and click on the "Favorite Projects" archive. Under Bedroom, click on "Power of Paint Headboard ND0504."

American Tradition,
Cool Violet
#1001-6C, flat

American Tradition,
Pale Bloom
#7002-8, semi-gloss

American Tradition,
Lilac Whisper
#4003-9A, satin

American Tradition,
Cabin Plank
#2011-10, semi-gloss

American Tradition,
Purpling Dawn
#1001-6B, semi-gloss

step 2

decorating

magnetic stripes

There is no limit to the number of effects you can get with stripes. For a subtle look, use a tone-on-tone scheme, like this combination of soft greens. Consider shades of pink or salmon in a girl's room.

Here's the nifty extra touch in this project: Alternating stripes are magnetic. Magnetic primer turns the surface into a bulletin board or art gallery without a single hole in the wall. (Be sure not to put a computer or other electronic storage device adjacent to the magnetic surfaces.)

Step 1: Apply your first color to the entire wall. Repeat if needed and let it dry.

Step 2: Using a tape measure or ruler held horizontally, measure and mark the stripe widths across the wall (the stripes on our wall are 12 inches wide).

Step 3: For straight stripes, use a laser level, as shown, to mark the vertical lines. Tape ✕'s on the stripes that will not be magnetic. Apply tape to the outside edges of the lines of the stripes that will be magnetic. With your thumb or a putty knife, burnish the edge of the tape along the side that will be painted, to prevent paint from seeping underneath.

Step 4: Use a roller to apply a coat of magnetic primer to the stripes being painted. Allow to dry, and then repeat. Additional coats will increase the magnetic attraction.

Step 5: With a clean roller, paint over the primer with your second color. Let it dry, and then repeat with additional coats as needed.

Step 6: Carefully remove the tape. Attach artwork to the wall using heavy-duty magnets.

step 3

step 4

step 5

step 6

Lowe's list

materials
- drop cloth
- tape measure or ruler
- laser level
- painter's tape
- putty knife
- roller kit
- ³⁄₈-inch roller covers
- box of rags

paint
- first color (American Tradition, Hubbell House Tamarisk #6004-5C, satin)
- magnetic latex primer (Rust-Oleum, #115535)*
- second color, for stripes (American Tradition, Homestead Resort Spa Green #6004-5B, satin)

Skill level: Beginner

Rough cost estimate: $110**

Rough time estimate: 2 days (depending on size of your room)

*Selection varies by market.
**Does not include labor costs or applicable taxes, which vary by market.

Yellow-toned maple cabinets make a fresh, vibrant contrast to **pastel blue** walls. Neutral-colored slate backsplash tiles, self-stick vinyl flooring, a bamboo shade, and a graphite gray laminate countertop add lots of visual texture without overpowering the color scheme.

colorful contrasts

Pastels can be very energizing when you use two or more complementary colors together. Consider combining them in a floral pattern on a sofa. Or imagine using a series of pastels—mint green, lemon yellow, and soft pink—on the walls of adjoining rooms. Hold the scheme together by painting all the trim white.

▲ Pairing **pastel blue and yellow** creates a gender-neutral foundation for a nursery. The airiness of blue coupled with the warmth of yellow always makes a joyful combination and a guaranteed success for a child's room. The white wood trim, along with other white elements, accentuates the pale yellow on the walls.

▶ There are **double contrasts** in this cozy window-seat nook: pale blue and pink in the stencils and accent fabrics, greens and yellows in the paint and primary fabrics. The variety of colors has a dynamic effect on the soft, welcoming palette.

American Tradition,
Willow Wind
#6004-3B

American Tradition,
Sandstone Gray
7004-18, semi-gloss

Contrasting hues from a beach-inspired palette set a relaxing mood in this living room. While all the color is soft, there is plenty of it, from the walls and painted chest to the ottoman and pillows. To play up the contrast and add energy to the cool blue, the homeowner used just a few accents of warm yellow and pink. Here are some tips to help you pull off a similar look.

CHOOSE A MAIN WALL COLOR AND ADD ACCENT HUES The soft pastel blue on the walls pairs with a light green in the interior of the glass-fronted cabinets.

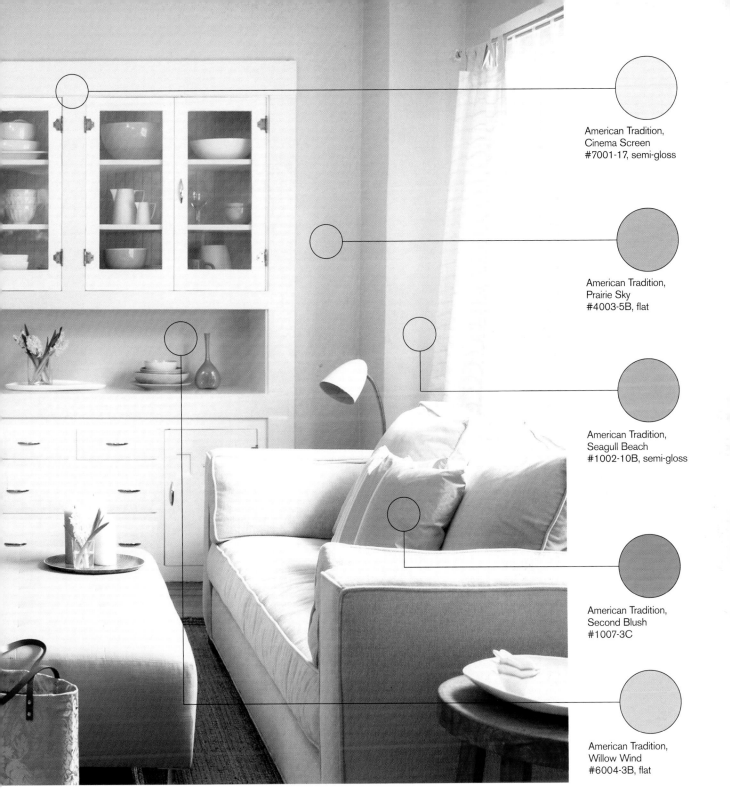

American Tradition,
Cinema Screen
#7001-17, semi-gloss

American Tradition,
Prairie Sky
#4003-5B, flat

American Tradition,
Seagull Beach
#1002-10B, semi-gloss

American Tradition,
Second Blush
#1007-3C

American Tradition,
Willow Wind
#6004-3B, flat

CALL OUT ARCHITECTURAL FEATURES Use a different accent color (here, a grayish beige) around the windows to give them more prominence.

USE A CONTRASTING TRIM COLOR The homeowner painted the doors and casing of the built-in cabinets a soft white to make them stand out against the blue walls. The baseboards are a flattering off-white.

ADD COORDINATED COLORS ON FURNISHINGS The pale blue ottoman matches the blue walls, while the sandy-colored sofa and chair go with the neutral trim. The green of the cabinet interior, picked up in the drawers of the chest, warms up the cool blue.

BALANCE COLORS AND ADD TEXTURE The hues in the throw pillows play off one another and distribute color around the room. The delicate fabrics contrast with the coarsely woven, multitoned sisal rug.

▲ A colorful mix of pastel ceramic tiles, laid in a **mosaic pattern** on countertop, backsplash, and floor, adds a delightfully un-expected flair to a gray kitchen.

◀ Floral **print** shades and a patterned tablecloth soften the corner angles of a pretty peach breakfast nook and enliven the morning scene.

Texture and Pattern in a Pastel Scheme

While pastels are wonderfully relaxing, you may want to avoid creating an atmosphere that is too subdued. The trick is to introduce a good mix of texture and pattern into the decorating scheme. If you are working with a single color, combine several patterns and textures for visual interest. When working with a more complex palette, unite it by using a single, or similar, texture or pattern.

◀ You can use **accessories** to add not only color but also texture and pattern. One benefit is that they're easily replaced as trends change or your individual taste evolves. These whimsical pastel accessories introduce a fun and playful style to a room.

▲ **Hand-painted art** on a wall or ceiling personalizes a space while adding pattern. Here the blossoming willow gives depth to a corner, while a grass border sprouts along the top of the wainscot. If you don't feel artistically inclined, you can hire a decorative painter to work this type of magic on your walls, or take advantage of the many wallpaper borders and stencils available.

▲ **Pale sorbet green** on the walls of this bedroom flatters the architectural details and echoes the greenery visible through the large window. But the cool palette requires some pattern—the green batik print used for the window treatments and pillow shams—and texture in the fabrics to give it a lift.

▶ In remodeling this bath, the homeowners wanted a color that would welcome them each morning. They found what they were looking for with this soft periwinkle blue. But the success of the scheme results from the **finishing details.** The texture of the glass-block shower wall and the white beaded-board wainscot, the shine of the stainless steel hardware, and the pattern of the limestone-like porcelain floor tiles all keep the room from becoming too pale or ethereal.

◀ A headboard covered in yellow **plaid** wallpaper pops out on a pastel blue wall, showing that you don't need to cover an entire wall in pattern to decorate with flair. Framed floral motifs from coordinating wallpaper are a nice natural-form contrast to the graphic design.

Paintable textured wallpaper adds depth and dimension to a room. This kind of subtle pattern unobtrusively breaks up a flat expanse of color.

wallcoverings

Wallcoverings are one of the best ways to introduce pattern and texture to any room. And the wallpapers available today are more stylish and easier to hang than ever before. You can get wallpaper in a wide range of patterns and colors, including new paintable textured replications (above) and coverings that simulate painted faux finishes (right).

Wallpaper with a natural look—such as grass cloth, linen, flocked velvet, or foil—is also back in style and can be found in a wide range of colors and textures. Many wallpaper companies offer preassembled collections of paper and fabrics, making it easy for you to layer a room—a border over a wall pattern, perhaps—or coordinate your window treatment with your walls.

To keep wallpaper from overwhelming a space, use it on one wall as an accent. Or paint the bottom third of a wall a solid color, run a border or chair rail above that, and hang wallpaper above the border. You can create matching accessories by using wallpaper to cover a wastebasket or a child's toy box.

For more information on how to hang wallpaper, or to view products, log onto **Lowes.com** and search with the keyword "wallpaper."

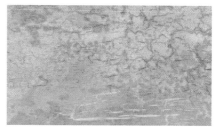

Village,
Pattern 5813980,
#164733*

Imperial,
Pattern CS8254,
#70731*

Wall Trends
International,
Pattern 30614610,
#98581*

*Selections vary by market.

wall's width (feet) \ wall's height (feet)	8	9	10	11	12
6	3	3	3	4	5
8	3	4	4	5	6
10	5	5	5	6	7
12	5	5	5	7	8
14	5	5	7	7	8
16	7	7	8	8	9
18	7	8	8	8	10
20	8	8	9	10	11
22	9	9	10	11	12
24	9	9	10	12	13

shop smart

estimating wallpaper needs

When working with wallpaper, you'll want to purchase all you'll need at one time. You're more likely to get all the rolls from the same dye lot, avoiding major color variations. Use this chart to estimate the number of single rolls for walls of specific heights and widths. (You can also visit **Lowes.com/calculators** for wallpaper and other project calculators.) Measure carefully and round up to the nearest foot. Subtract half a roll for each standard door or window opening. Ask a Lowe's employee to help you adjust for your repeat length (the repeat length, generally printed on the back of the roll, is the distance between one design element and the next occurrence of that element in a pattern).

▶ **Grass cloth** softens the walls of an entry hall in a modern house. Natural grass cloth is best used in a low-traffic, low-moisture area. Vinyl printed to look like grass cloth will mimic the textured effect but is more durable and easier to clean.

earth
tones

The rich mid-tones and deep tones take their cues from the earth: dark greens found in foliage; blends of reds, browns, and yellows from a region's native soil; blues from stone and the sky. There is no better way to connect your living **environment** with the great outdoors than by decorating with these lush, natural shades.

You may feel that mid-tones and deep tones are too dark for your home, but look through this chapter to see how they can enrich your interior setting. Earth tones not only create a **sophisticated** atmosphere but also mix well with other natural furnishings and finishes, such as wood, glass, fiber, and stone. Stronger than the gentle neutrals and pastels, they are also **easy** to live with. If you prefer to use natural colors in light doses, try one of the small projects in this chapter. They'll let you add just a touch of **deep color** to your decor. Whether you are creating a textured wall or making headboards out of drapery panels, these small projects offer a big chance to experiment with color.

Slate blue is a sophisticated color for kitchen cabinetry. These cabinets are teamed with a deep yellow backsplash and orange wood tones to guarantee this room is as cheerful as it is elegant.

Mid-tones and Deep Tones

Mid-tones and deep tones are more saturated in color than neutrals and richer in tone than pastels. While a pastel hue is a pure color mixed with white, mid-tones and deep tones are colors combined with either black or their direct complements. Two complements mixed in equal proportions create a shade of gray. In uneven proportions, the dominant color becomes deeper and richer, and since it's closer to neutral, it's more comfortable to live with.

These natural colors are so popular because, like a shady forest glen or a dark mountain lake, they create a tranquil, embracing atmosphere that is easy on the eye. With their depth of color, they also make striking accents in a neutral or pastel scheme. Mid-tones and deep tones are like color seen in shadow rather than in bright sunlight. Think olive or forest green rather than grass green or chartreuse; slate or dusty blue instead of sky blue or turquoise; ochre or mustard in place of lemon yellow; burgundy or rosy brown as opposed to apple red.

Because deeper colors can make a room feel smaller than light ones do, these tones are especially effective in large areas or in any room where you want to create a sense of intimacy or coziness. Brick reds, terra-cottas, mahoganies, and mustard yellows will make a space feel warmer. Consider using them in kitchens, dining areas, and family rooms. Deep and olive greens and slate blues will calm a space, so they're particularly well used in bedrooms and formal living areas.

◄ **Natural green** complements the tones of wood flooring and ceiling. The color also adds depth to the wall of shelves.

◄ A corner of a study becomes a focal point when splashed with **rich color.** The three primaries—red, yellow, and blue—are always sophisticated when used in their deeper tones.

▶ **Deep red and blue** work well together because of their similar tones, providing a stylish balance of hot and cool. To enrich the scheme, the leather and wood furniture pieces are a darker shade of burgundy.

◀ A bold terra-cotta red frames the fireplace wall, which is made of cast concrete tinted olive gray. The strong color contrasts reinforce the room's spare, **contemporary** lines.

▼ A deep plum red highlights one wall in a Victorian-inspired master bath remodel. The ceiling tiles were glazed a dark burgundy to lend a classic feel that's in keeping with the traditional **Victorian** decor.

Pairing Earth Tones with Architectural Styles

Earth tones are particularly suited to casual architectural styles that focus on the use of natural materials, such as the Arts and Crafts style, identified by its connection with the materials and colors of the local environment. Both rustic and Southwest styles take their color cues from their regional landscapes. Early Colonial architecture, with its emphasis on wood trim and wall paneling, also employed these colors—the more faded tones of deep blues, mustards, greens, and reds. Later traditional styles were less interested in the link with nature. The complex schemes of the Victorian style did use deep red and eggplant but rarely blues or yellows. In any contemporary setting, you can add earth tones with confidence, as the main attraction or as an accent.

▼ Every color in this formal **Arts and Crafts** sitting room evokes nature, from the colorwashed green walls to the brown leather sofa and dark-stained wood cabinets and trim. Notice how the homeowners have painted the inside of the cabinet a mid-tone blue to increase its sense of depth.

Color Schemes
That Work

Of all the various color possibilities, mid-tones and deep tones are the easiest to imagine in combination because we see a spectrum of earth tones every time we step outside. When outdoors, note the many deep colors visible. Then list all your favorite combinations. A garden magazine is a great place to start if you want to stay indoors to research these colors.

schemes that blend

Deep colors are so rich that any single-color scheme will be enticing. If you like green—one of today's most popular hues—take a walk through a garden and notice how many different shades exist side by side, from yellowy olives to the bluest sage. Look out on a lake for inspiration in combining shades of blue. For reds, look at the varieties of color in a row of clay pots. For oranges and deep yellows, consider a maple tree as it changes color in fall.

▶ A deep, **dusty blue** sets off a neutral brown cabinet, highlighting the collection of green and plum-colored glassware.

◀ **Marine blue** is a handsome background for a bright and jazzy focal point. The homeowner lit—and lightened—the corner by turning two ordinary five-light bath bar fixtures on end. A dimmer switch allows the ambience to modulate from soft glow to theatrical.

▲ A **deep, earthy orange** blends well with furnishings made from wood, stone, and metal. To keep this warm color from overwhelming the room, it was used on only one wall and flanked with a neutral color that matches the lighter tones in the stone floor.

◄ A dark yellow-green is **fresh and inviting** in a formal living room. The shiny texture of the gold picture frames, chair frame, and candlestick holders punches up the color scheme.

▲ In another blending scheme, an existing **red brick wall** sets the theme for this polished kitchen. Cherry cabinetry with a Bordeaux stain picks up the earth tones, providing all the color this handsome space requires. Because all other surfaces are neutral, it's possible to add a touch of any contrasting color, such as the blue dishes and glassware.

▶ A blue-green wall pairs with an olive green one to create a soothingly **elegant blend.** Gilded accessories add richness. Notice how the blue, green, and gold scheme derives from the colors in the still-life painting.

dressed-up headboard

An easy way to enrich a limited color palette is to use fabric in unique ways. The wine-colored cloth backdrop is a piece of simple sophistication created with a drapery panel and rod. Measure up from the floor behind the bed to a height slightly less than the length of your selected drapery panel. Center and install a curtain rod above the bed using the hardware that comes with it. Hang the drapery panel on the rod. Use one panel for a twin bed, or combine multiple panels to add color or to fit a larger bed.

strokes of genius

For a quick transformation, painting is one of the least expensive ways to update your decor. It's also something you can do yourself without much experience. Easy-to-use products, such as helpful trim tools, souped-up rollers, cordless sprayers, and combination sets, will lend a professional look to your job.

roll-on style

Choose a power roller to cover a room quickly. The device draws paint from the can through a tube to the roller. You'll find a long-handled roller with paint-dispensing capabilities makes for less mess and physical work when you're painting ceilings.

spray-on style

Cordless sprayers provide a quick-drying, even finish to textured or uneven surfaces that can be hard to paint with a brush or roller. Whether you're covering a piece of wicker furniture, a bumpy sprayed ceiling, or a louvered closet door, a sprayer can help you achieve a professional look in less time.

around the edges

Special trim brushes and painter's tape can steady your strokes around windows, doors, and moulding. Edgers with built-in paint dispensers allow for faster application and, in some situations, eliminate the need for tape. All these tools will help you paint a room as you would a page in a coloring book: outline first, then fill in.

convenient touch-up kits

Keep a touch-up kit on hand for when you need to fix a small section of wall or furniture. These kits, which let you store several paint colors, include three containers, a brush, a roller, a filling funnel, and a storage case. Simply pour leftover paint into the reusable, airtight containers and then use the brush or attachable roller to easily touch up any area.

one-stop shopping

Instead of purchasing a separate tray and bucket, try a tray and bucket in one to help with cleaner mixing and pouring. Packaged kits offer a combination of trays and applicators, including foam brushes, rollers, trim tools, and extension handles.

colorful contrasts

If you like deep colors and want to create a bit of excitement, nature provides all the inspiration you need for great combinations. Forest green trees against a deep blue sky. Deep yellow grasses against rich red clay soil. Green moss and orange lichen on the side of a brown boulder. There's no end to the possibilities when you're dealing with this earthy color set.

▶ A simple blue-and-orange scheme—rich blue mosaic tiles and granite with orange-hued cabinetry—works well because the two colors are perfect **complements**. A splash of green from the painted chair contributes a fresh accent color.

▼ Pairing two contemporary colors, such as pastel violet and the earth tone teal, on adjoining walls gives the antique bed, bench, and chair **a modern setting.** The redwood ceiling warms up what would be a cool color scheme on its own.

▲ **Shades of sand and sea** are mimicked on the walls and floor of this modern home. The beachy tones of the maple cabinets, floor tiles, and rattan chairs provide a nice contrast to the deep ocean blue of the concrete floor and walls.

◀ This scheme borrows its hues from the changing **colors of fall** foliage—from green to red and yellow to russet brown. The green window trim blends with the foliage outside, enhancing the connection between indoors and out. The sunny yellow creates a fun mood.

▲ Deep terra-cotta motivates and inspires the creative mind in this cozy office space. The yellow-toned wood floor and cabinets, the green plants, and the dark beams offer an attractive **contrast.**

▶ The **primaries**—red, blue, and yellow—work successfully here without being overpowering, as they appear in darker earth tones. Using different proportions is critical when you have multiple colors in strong hues. Here the red and blue balance each other, while the ochre yellow serves as an accent. The cream color of the ceiling extends down the walls to the picture rails and window frames for a more spacious feeling.

▲ A screened porch is an ideal space for incorporating earth tones, and **contrasting reds, greens, and browns** work especially well here. This is a prime example of how pattern and texture add to the overall decor.

◄ Using **complementary red and green** in midtones and deep tones keeps this space from overheating, while the yellow tones of the wood cabinetry soften the palette. With this organic color scheme, stainless steel (usually sleek and modern) takes on a warmer, earthier feel.

shining a light on color
experiment with different
bulbs and shades to find
the ones that shed the
most flattering light

The way a color is lighted affects the way it
appears. Most light in your home is artificial,
and its color varies. The fixture itself is one
factor, but the biggest variable is the type of
bulb you use.

Light bulbs have five basic features. Each bulb has a **wattage.**
Check the correct wattage for your fixture and choose the appropriate bulb to avoid overheating. **Lumens** denotes the amount of
light—the more lumens, the brighter the light. Compare how long
bulbs last by checking the number of **hours.** Bulbs have different
bases—medium, candelabra, and bi-pin are among the most
common. The last element is the **bulb type**: incandescent, halogen, fluorescent, or compact fluorescent.

fluorescent
Standard fluorescent
bulbs are created
specifically for fluores-
cent fixtures, so they
have pin-type bases.
Fluorescents now
come in colors closer
to natural light. "Day-
light" and "sunshine"
options simulate out-
door light and work well in low-light situations or where true
color is important. Fluorescent bulbs last an exceptionally long
time and are available in several shapes.

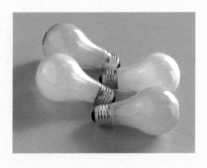

incandescent
Typically the least
expensive type, incan-
descent bulbs come
in a variety of styles,
including globes for
vanities, tube shapes
for under cabinets,
and floodlights for
recessed fixtures. The
common "soft white" light is good for general-purpose lighting
and will intensify yellows, reds, and browns but will tend to dull
the cooler colors. "Daylight" bulbs simulate natural light, filtering
out yellow tones and producing a crisp light for true colors. Soft
pink flatters skin tones. Clear or faceted bulbs make crystal
sparkle and are good choices for chandeliers.

compact
fluorescent
(CFL)
For the most energy
efficiency, use com-
pact fluorescent
bulbs. They are in-
deed smaller than
regular fluorescents;
because of their stan-

dard base, they fit most conventional fixtures. They come in various wattages as well as a range of shapes, including spiral,
tubular, globe, decorative, and reflector. CFLs offer longevity and
efficiency: A CFL bulb uses two-thirds less energy than a standard incandescent and lasts up to 10 times longer, providing
you considerable savings in both money and energy. Available in
soft white for general-purpose lighting and in "daylight" for a
crisp tone that is great for reading and task lighting, they come
close to providing the warmth of incandescent bulbs.

halogen
Halogen bulbs cost
more than incandescent
ones but also last up to
three times longer. They
produce almost 50 per-
cent more light for the
same amount of energy,
which allows you to pur-
chase a lower wattage

and save on energy costs. Halogen bulbs produce the brightest,
purest light, which makes tasks like reading easier. They are effective for highlighting artwork, since they render truer, more natural
color. Halogen bulbs are available with a normal base in various
bulb shapes as well as spots and floodlights. They also come with
a pin-type base for special fixtures such as torchères.

A dimmer switch gives you greater control over the amount
of light in a room, affecting both color and mood. Low light
darkens colors, while a higher level will make colors lighter
and brighter and sharpen contrasts. Dimmer switches work
well with incandescent, halogen, and CFL bulbs. In addition to replacing a standard switch with a dimmer, you can
also control a light with a remote-control dimmer.

Texture and Pattern with Earth Tones

From the rough texture of bark on a brown tree trunk to the shiny green of new leaves to the mottled matte shades in boulders, texture and pattern are everywhere. Just look to your natural environment to understand the effect of these qualities on the overall design scheme.

▲ A rug, artful window shades, and accent pillows in contrasting colors introduce **contemporary pattern** in this relaxing bedroom retreat. The dark blue walls recede, letting the window and floor art take center stage.

▶ **Painted furniture** adds color and texture to a room without making any permanent changes. This tall cabinet was built in a weekend from an unfinished bookcase and two window shutters. The bookcase was painted a dark sage green. The shutter doors were brushed with a semitransparent stain slightly lighter than the paint. The contrasting interior is a sunny yellow.

▲ Tile offers a great way to add **both pattern and texture** to a room. Deep-toned accent tiles in reds, blues, browns, and ochres are mixed with field tiles of tumbled marble to give this neutral-colored kitchen real style.

▶ A wall of cabinets provides eye-catching pattern in a modern kitchen. The **rectangular shapes** in deeper shades of blue, olive green, yellow-green, and cream are made with solid-color plastic laminates. Breaking the long wall into sections, the pattern visually reduces what could be an overpowering presence. It even camouflages the refrigerator. A few bright purple panels add excitement.

▲ The depth of
midnight blue
imbues this con-
temporary bath
with calm and
serenity. **Pattern**—
the simple border
of darker tiles
around the walls—
adds an energizing
touch.

torn wallpaper

Wallpaper is a great product for adding both pattern and texture to a surface. In addition to being applied conventionally, it can be torn and stuck on in pieces, offering the same look as a beautiful faux finish but with less cost and in less time. The wallpaper is as simple to remove as it is to apply. Just use a sponge to spread warm water to your surface, then pull the pieces off.

Step 1: Tear pre-pasted wallpaper into irregular shapes and sizes.
Step 2: Immerse the pasted side of each piece in a water-filled container, such as a bucket, allowing excess water to drip into the container.
Step 3: Apply the pieces to the surface. Wipe off the excess water and allow the paper to dry.

For more ideas on how to use torn wallpaper to add texture and color to a room, visit LowesCreativeIdeas.com/projwallpaper.asp.

step 1

step 2

step 3

▲ **Pattern** is created by the lines of wood panels, dentil moulding at the tops of the walls, and a coffered ceiling, breaking up the expanse of cool, tranquil blue-green.

▶ When the color of a window treatment matches the walls, it's important to **vary the texture** to avoid monotony. Cellular shades in a deep olive green provide an attractive texture as well as privacy and insulation.

textured wall color

To enliven a solid-color wall, try a faux finish. There are many types of faux finishes, utilizing a variety of techniques and tools. There are also a number of textured paints that can replicate the look of suede, metal, granite, or shiny quartz.

This project gives a dining room wall a fresco treatment that looks like aged plaster. The homeowner-painter created her own version of a classic Italian technique by mixing several colors of paint with spackling compound. You can simplify the process by using a textured paint called Venetian plaster, which has the color already mixed in. Practice before you start working on your walls. Remember that the result should look like naturally aged plaster, an effect that is perfectly imperfect.

Step 1: Choose paint in your desired colors. A dark, a medium, and a light shade work well. For a 12- x 14-foot room, you'll use roughly 1 gallon plus 1 quart of the darkest shade, plus 1 quart each of the other two hues.

Step 2: Perfect your technique on hardboard or ¼-inch plywood before starting on the walls. When you're ready, prepare the walls. After making sure they are clean and free of debris, wipe them down with a damp cloth and let them dry. Fill any nail holes with putty. Let dry, then sand smooth. Next apply painter's tape around any trim.

Step 3: Use a roller to apply the darkest shade of paint on the wall. This will be your basecoat. (Tip: When blending several layers of paint, always begin with the darkest color and then work up to the lighter tones.)

Step 4: Wearing latex gloves, put some spackling compound in each empty container and add one color of paint to each, stirring as you go. The ratio will be approximately 1 quart paint to 1 gallon spackling compound. Mix until you get the color you desire, making note of the exact ratio you used, in case you need more later. (If you use textured paint, such as Venetian plaster, you can eliminate this step.)

Step 5: Working in a 2½-foot-square area, trowel on the darkest hue of spackling compound mixture. Wipe the trowel clean and spread on the second color mixture while the wall is wet. Blend with the trowel.

Step 6: Wipe the trowel clean and layer on the third color mixture while the wall is still wet. Continue working in small areas around the room, layering and blending as you go.

Step 7: Let the wall dry, then sand it to knock off loose pieces and jagged edges. Remove the painter's tape. You can brush on polyurethane to seal the finish if desired (recommended if you're using this treatment in a bath).

Lowe's list

materials
- 3 containers, 1 gallon each, interior/ exterior spackling compound
- 3 mixing containers, about 2 gallons each
- rags
- painter's tape
- latex gloves
- paint roller
- paint stirrers
- trowel
- drop cloth
- 220-grit sandpaper
- paintbrush (optional)
- polyurethane (optional)

paint
- 1 gallon plus 1 quart dark paint (American Tradition, Foamy Sea #283-2, eggshell)
- 1 quart medium paint (American Tradition, Delicate Cloud #282A-2, eggshell)
- 1 quart light paint (American Tradition, Spring Eve #316-3, eggshell)

Skill level: Beginner

Rough cost estimate: $100*

Rough time estimate: 1 day

*Does not include applicable taxes, which may vary by market, or the cost of tools.

step 5

step 6

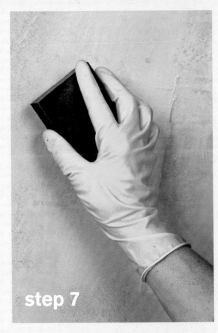
step 7

bold, bright color

b Bright, strong color brings exuberance to your interior spaces, whether you splash it across every wall or limit it to furnishings and accessories. You could, for instance, spice up the kitchen with a set of cobalt blue pendant lamps over the island, hang color-rich floral drapes at a bedroom window, or cover a family-room floor in one of today's sassy hues. Using colors like these, you can have fun creating a signature look that is all your own.

Since bright color is powerful, this chapter focuses on how to use it in the right combinations and proportions so as not to overwhelm a space. The latest brights include the luscious hues of cherry red, lemon yellow, and apple green as well as less traditional shades of turquoise blue, grape purple, hibiscus pink, and fiery tangerine orange. It's best to limit these stimulating colors to areas where you want to promote activity, such as family rooms, dining rooms, kitchens, and kids' rooms. Bold color in a bedroom or bath can help you jump-start your day, but note that it can be a bit too energizing in these rooms for people who have trouble relaxing or getting to sleep.

A **dynamic color** palette plays off modern architecture and brings a joyful spirit to this small family home. Neutral furnishings and accessories work well with such strong color on the walls.

Pairing Bright Colors
with Architectural Styles

A vibrant palette feels fresh and up-to-date; it's almost always right with contemporary design. In moderate doses, it can modernize a dated room or give a new edge to a traditional one. And while these colors are not usually used with such casual styles as cottage and Arts and Crafts, they are practically the essence of Southwest style.

▼ This is a great example of how an unconventional mix of intense colors creates a **cheerful and ultra-contemporary** dining area. Bright yellow dominates, with accents of purple, raspberry, and coral. While there is no real method to the madness, these wild contrasts are tempered by the eye-catching lines and texture of the neutral gray metal staircase. To continue the playful theme, the homeowners store pens, collected throughout their travels, in an assortment of colorful mugs.

▲ Against a backdrop of white walls and cabinetry, brightly colored Mexican tile underscores the Spanish Colonial style of this **casual** kitchen. The colors, reflecting the strong sun, sky, and earth of the Southwestern landscape, both define and enhance the architecture.

▶ The intensity of this periwinkle blue, drawn from the Claude Monet print on the wall, helps bring a **traditional** bedroom up to date. Note how the use of white as a contrast makes the color stand out.

A staggered pattern in two coordinating hues of **bright lavender** adds flair to this wall, accented by the lines of the black accessories. A neutral yellow floor balances the strong color.

Color Schemes That Work

Bright colors are impossible to ignore, so when you select a bold palette, you want to make sure of two things: that you love each color and that you have the right balance of colors. Using several in equal amounts will be the most exciting, but this also ups the visual tension in the room. You'll probably find it easier to live with vivid colors when you vary either their shades or their proportions, making one the dominant color and the others accents. The characteristics of a color, such as the mood it creates or how it affects a room's sense of space, will be more pronounced when it is used in its brightest shades, so be ready for some results that pack a punch.

schemes that blend

A single brilliant color stands out vividly and can create drama all on its own. For that reason, many bright color schemes are paired with white: bright blue curtains in a white room, or white trim on a bright yellow wall. For multicolored schemes, the most harmonious are those that mix hues sitting next to each other on the color wheel (see page 22).

▶ **Vivid yellow** contrasts with adjacent white surfaces to magnify this bedroom's sunlit quality. Wood trim and ceiling panels with softer orange tones complement the bright color.

▼ **A playful shade** of turquoise makes every day feel like clear skies ahead in this combination home office and hobby room. The vibrant hue, along with white wood trim, ceiling, and furnishings, brightens and lightens the space. Note the wood chair, painted white and trimmed in the same blue, with touches of bright color under the seat.

A back entry is a space that can handle bold color. Here bright shades of aqua and green jazz up an often overlooked space, welcoming the kids home. The two **fun colors** mix well with yellowish tan floor tiles. A tan wall to the left of the door is a neutral backdrop for the blue peg-and-shelf unit and serves as a calm transition to the nearby family room.

eye-catchers

Create a focal point in any room or hallway with a simple paint treatment. At left, a 36-inch dark aqua square on a light aqua wall creates a geometric background for a round mirror. To duplicate this color square, first paint the wall a light color. We used American Tradition, Lake Breeze #5007-7B. Measure and lightly mark a 36-inch square. Tape off the edges with painter's tape and paint inside the tape with a darker shade (in this case, American Tradition, Turquoise Tint #5006-10B). Let it dry. Center and mount a 28-inch round mirror inside the square.

In the example below, orange paint on a fuchsia wall makes a frame, interestingly intersected by a bracketless metallic shelf. To duplicate this color frame, measure and lightly mark a 42-inch square. Measure 4 inches in from all sides and mark again, creating a border. Tape off the edges with painter's tape and paint the border in a hue that contrasts with the wall color. We used American Tradition Signature Colors Laura Ashley: Fuchsia #218, eggshell, on the wall and Pumpkin 5 #605, satin, for the border. Let it dry. Install a 36-inch bracketless shelf so that it overlaps the border by about 8 inches. Place an accent piece on the shelf.

colorful contrasts

When you think of bright contrasts, the most obvious are the primaries—red, blue, and yellow—used in full force. But there are lots of other combinations that are sophisticated and beautiful. It doesn't take much to create sparkle and pop when you mix these vibrant hues. Vary the proportions to keep the scheme from being overwhelming.

◀ **Big colors** fire up a small galley kitchen. A vivid red, blue, and tan ceramic tile backsplash becomes the room's focal point. Note how the hot red dominates even though it covers a relatively small area. Yellow-toned maple-veneer cabinets and a bright yellow wall reinforce the cheerful setting.

▼ For a fun and dynamic atmosphere in a children's bath, a blue countertop and tub deck contrast with the orange tones of the cabinetry and window moulding. Yellow tiles balance the **complementary blue and orange.**

◀ Pairing the cool freshness of a brilliant **violet blue** with the warm cheerfulness of bright yellow seems to expand this cottage living room beyond its small size. Neutral furnishings are the best option when you apply this much color to a room.

▼ A couple turned one wall of their joint home office into a focal point by painting it a **bright apple green,** a color that is both cheerful and invigorating. While the green is dominant, the scheme is in balance because of the red hardwood floor—a direct complement. To keep the room from being too bright—this is an office, after all—the design is completed with neutral gray and black furnishings and accessories.

So much bright color works in this nursery because a single tone is dominant, from the walls to the wood furniture. Small **contrasting accents** in the rug, curtains, and linens break up the field of orange.

▼ Energizing a corner of a family room, these versions of pink and green are anything but sedate. Whip up this quick, easy look by painting unfinished cabinetry pink and white, with green "panels" painted freehand on the door and drawer fronts. Add a green laminate countertop and insert green glass tiles in the white backsplash for **a snappy look.**

American Tradition,
Poppy Field #1006-1C,
eggshell

American Tradition,
Gentle Pasture #6003-4A,
semi-gloss

American Tradition,
Pale Bloom #7002-8,
semi-gloss

◄ Instead of gutting the kitchen and starting over, the owners of this home used color to transform the room. **Purplish red and yellow** floor tiles became the basis for their palette. The old cabinets were painted to match, making the bolder red a sideshow rather than the main event.

► Because it's used on just one wall, bright color jazzes up a small dining area without overwhelming it. The **lime green** wall reflects the color of the grass outside the tall glass doors. A complementary red countertop adds zing.

decorating

a painted table

Add a bold splash of color to any room with a piece of painted wood furniture. To build this table from scratch, follow these easy steps.

Step 1: Lay the pine panel with its best side facedown. Because the panel is made of laminated pine strips, the manufacturer's "glue lines" cross it at regular intervals. Mark the midpoint of a glue line. Using a framing square, draw a line from this mark perpendicular to the glue line, then extend it to the outside edges of the panel. Find the center point of the line you just drew and then draw a second line perpendicular to it, starting at the midpoint and extending to the edges. This divides the panel into quarters. On each of the four lines, about 2 inches from the edge, mark the placement of a mounting plate.

Step 2: Drill the holes needed to attach the mounting plates.

Step 3: Prime and lightly sand the panel and the four legs. Paint the legs. Firmly attach the four mounting plates to the underside of the panel using the predrilled holes.

Step 4: Paint the entire tabletop in the lightest color (here it's the same blue used on the legs). Add a second coat if necessary. Next paint contrasting-colored stripes, using painter's tape to create straight edges between the stripes. (Here bright green, pink, and another shade of blue are used.) Allow it to dry.

Step 5: Add a furniture glide to the end of each table leg. Screw a table leg into each mounting plate.

step 1

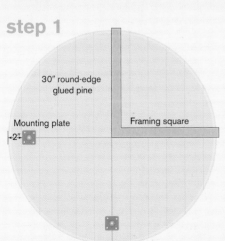

30" round-edge glued pine

Mounting plate Framing square

2"

Lowe's list

materials
- 1 (⁵⁄₄-inch-thick) 30-inch round-edge glued ponderosa pine panel*
- 4 straight-top mounting plates
- 4 (28-inch) Parsons table legs
- primer
- paint (American Tradition: Aqua Ocean #5505-10A; Cool Rain #5005-10C; Frosty Berry #1003-1B; Martian #6007-8C; high gloss)
- painter's tape
- 1 package of nail-on furniture glides

tools
- tape measure
- pencil
- power drill/driver and bit set
- framing square
- hammer
- sandpaper

Skill level: Beginner

Rough cost estimate: $80**

Rough time estimate: 1–2 days

*Availability varies by market.
**Does not include applicable taxes, which vary by market, or the cost of tools.

Texture and Pattern with a Bright Palette

You don't need a lot of pattern and texture to energize a bright scheme, but they add variety and can break up a solid field of color. The examples here show what happens when you let yourself go a little wild.

▲ A mixture of strong colors and patterns gives energy to a small room. Limiting the scheme to two colors helps unite the variety of **checks, florals, and stripes.**

◀ Lay your color on the floor. A room's main focal point, this **freestyle** pattern on a concrete floor was created with water-based paints. A decorative treatment like this, appropriate to an entry hall or playroom in a contemporary home, can be painted over if tastes change.

Mosaic tiles provide a rainbow of color options. Here the home-owners used as many as they could to create shiny **stripes and color blocks** in a bath. With a few bright towels and a rubber ducky or two, this room not only welcomes kids in but makes bath time fun.

► Stenciling is an easy and inexpensive way to add pattern to a wall or furniture. This fun **letter-and-number pattern** uses house address stencils from the hardware department. Join individual stencils in a straight line using painter's tape, secure the stencil to the wall with painter's tape, and then dab on paint lightly with a sponge. The three bright greens that make up this design are held in check by the neutral background.

▼ Orange squares painted over a yellow base create a **checkerboard pattern,** welcoming guests into this lighthearted home. It is a treatment that might be overwhelming in a larger space but works perfectly in an entry. A wavy-legged table adds to the fun.

▶ An assortment of colorful collectibles arranged on bracketless shelves softens the impact of a wall of strong fuchsia by superimposing various **shapes and patterns.** These unrelated items work so well together because they all include one common color: blue.

◀ Here the impact of a powerful color is softened by patterns and other hues—chiefly a complementary blue. Sticking with a **theme,** such as these polka dots and fish, helps control the variety of bold colors.

▶ Pattern and texture abound in this colorful kitchen. The theme is graphic, with rectangles, diamonds, and stripes covering nearly every surface. The creative blend of cherry, maple, and stained cabinets introduces **geometric pattern** in various tones of yellow, blue, and orange. Echoing the cabinets' block shapes are the windows and the inlaid border on the wood floor. Matte texture—the cabinetry and bright green laminate countertop—is balanced by shiny surfaces. Sinuous drawer pulls and an elliptical pendant lamp provide lively counterpoints to all the squared-off lines.

what a great idea

colorful **coasters**

Small additions can make large statements, like these decorative coasters made from inexpensive clay saucers. Scatter some across a dining or coffee table to add bright pattern to your decor. Begin by priming 4-inch saucers with acrylic paints. Add a base color and let it dry. Then personalize each coaster in contrasting colors with patterns such as polka dots, stripes, diamonds, squares, or free-form squiggles. Once the paint is dry, apply one or two coats of clear polyurethane.

In one woman's home, even the smallest decorative details are addressed with **color and pattern.** To dress up a staircase, she painted the tops and bottoms of 40 spindles in similar patterns and then applied magazine pages, business cards, and letters as decoupage to the center sections. She added wooden appliqués below the stair edges for even more color. So much pattern and color work when you limit them to small accent areas and paint your walls a single cool color.

Bright Accents for a Neutral Background

A little spot of bright color here and there does wonders for a neutral color scheme. There are numerous ways to introduce bright accents. Paint a single surface, include a few colored tiles in a neutral backsplash, add a single bright piece of furniture, or bring in some potted plants.

◀ This kitchen is a beautiful illustration of how to use **blocks of color** to enhance a largely neutral scheme. The red tiles and door and drawer fronts move the eye around the room, making it an energetic but not overly stimulating place to work.

▶ With **an array of colors** and styles to choose from, pendant lamps with glass globes provide striking accents in a neutral dining room or kitchen.

◀ **Bright artwork** works best against a neutral backdrop. In turn, what could be a very subdued room is enlivened by the vivid pieces.

► A bright aqua glass sink is an unexpected way to inject a **splash of color** into a neutral bath. The frosted glass adds a luminous glow.

◄ The green **foliage** of house-plants always enlivens a space. This vibrant palm adds interesting pattern as well as color in a neutral living room. While the plant takes a lead role, a faux rusted-iron planter plays its part, adding color and texture to the design.

► Red heats up almost any neutral scheme. Here red boxes and fabric baskets are **eye-popping** bright in a boy's tan, gray, and black bedroom.

Photo Credits

Left (L), Right (R), Top (T), Middle (M), Bottom (B)

Jean Allsopp: 11B, 41BR; **Christine E. Barnes:** 22–23; **Patrick Barta:** 27T; **Robbie Caponetto:** 50, 55TL, 59, 74–75, 108; **Van Chaplin:** 48–49B; **Gary Conaughton:** 116B; **Ken Druse:** 19T; **Cheryl Fenton:** 10, 36; **Brian Francis:** 94ML, BL, MR, BR; **Gloria Gale:** 26TL; **Tria Giovan:** 61B, 72B; **Laurey W. Glenn:** 28T, 32–33, 41T and BL, 64T; **Jay Graham:** 80; **John Granen:** 38T, 92B, 107T; **Ken Gutmaker:** 95T; **Jamie Hadley:** 6–7, 48BL, 58B, 83, 104, 110B, 116T, 118B; **Michael Hanson:** 37T, 46–47, 47TR, 62, 66–67 all, 89TR and BL, 94T, 124–125; **Margot Hartford:** 8–9, 24–25B; **Philip Harvey:** 19B; **Alex Hayden:** 69B; **James Frederick Housel:** 44L; **Bryan Johnson:** 37B, 38B, 40B, 49TR, 51, 53 all, 55TR and B, 73B, 84, 87, 88 both, 89TL and BR, 109T, 115, 123TR, 124B; **Muffy Kibbey:** 30–31, 82T; **Dennis Krukowski:** 58T; davidduncanlivingston.com: 91B, 96–97T, 97TR; **Peter Malinowski/InSite:** 105T; **Tim Maloney:** 102–103; **Sylvia Martin:** 82B, 119B; **E. Andrew McKinney:** 20–21, 26–27B, 99T, 117, 119T; **Mary E. Nichols:** 123B; **Geoffrey Nilsen:** 93B; **Wendy Nordeck:** 111T; **John O'Hagan:** 11T, 12, 13T, 14, 15T, 28B, 31T, 35, 39T, 43B, 45–46T, 52B, 54B, 63 both, 68, 74 both, 76 all, 86T, 92–93T, 98 all, 100–101 all, 106, 107B, 111B, 118T, 120BL, 120–121; **Bradley Olman:** 72T; **Chris Padgett:** 109B; **David Papazian:** 114B; **Robert Perron:** 17; **David Phelps:** 42, 90B; **Tom Rider:** 81T; **Lisa Romerein:** 25R, 77, 97B; **George Ross:** 16T; **Eric Roth Photography:** 90T; **Mark Samu:** 34; **Susan Seubert:** 114T; **Michael Skott:** 85TL; **Owen Stayner:** 61T; **Thomas J. Story:** 13B, 16B, 24–25T, 29B, 40T, 52T, 56–57, 64B, 70–71, 91T, 92T, 95B, 110T, 120T, 122; **Tim Street-Porter/Beateworks.com:** 39B; **Valspar:** 31B, 81B; **David Wakely:** 45B, 60, 86B; **Jessie Walker:** 105B; **Jason Wallis:** 15B, 18, 29T, 43T, 46L, 48–49T, 64–65, 113R; **Michele Lee Willson:** 69T, 72–73B, 112–113; **Karen Witynski:** 85TR; **Eric Zepeda:** 78–79.

Design Credits

Left (L), Right (R), Top (T), Middle (M), Bottom (B)

6–7: Gretchen Gibson and Jillann Wood/A Child's Eye View; **8–9:** Karen Austin, CKD, Creative Kitchens & Baths; **10:** Dede Lee; **11B:** Bill Allison, AIA, and Steve Hand, Allison Ramsay Architects; Steiner + Schelfe Design; **13B:** Architect: Eric Trabert & Associates; Annie Speck Interior Designs; **16T:** Kate Marchesini, Acorn Design Interiors; **16B:** Philip Volkmann, Barry & Volkmann Architects; **17:** Robert Orr; **20–21:** Architect: Richard Crandall; **24–25T:** Architect: Eric Trabert & Associates; Annie Speck Interior Designs; **24–25B:** Fox Design Group, Architects; interior design: Navarra Design, Inc.; **25R:** Sant Architects; **26T:** Lucy St. James; **26–27B:** D. Kimberly Smith/ Deer Creek Design; **28T:** Builder: Dale Burton; interior design: Jessie Davidson and Jennifer Chube; **29B:** Emma Star Jensen; **30:** DeMattei Construction; interior design: Ann Bertelsen and Leanne Holder; **32–33:** Carson Looney and Mark Jones, Looney Ricks Kiss Architects; Donna Brooks and Shona Binkowski, Brooks Interior Design; **34B:** Architect: Sam Schofield; **36:** Janine Regina and Denise Benson, Regina Interiors; **38T:** SkB Architects; **39B:** Steven Harby; **40T:** Architect: Dale Gardon Design; Tamm Jasper Interiors; **41BR:** Architect:

Barry Sugerman; **42:** Jim Davis; **44L:** Lane Williams Architects; **45B:** Janice Stone Thomas, ASID, CKD, Stone-Wood Design, Inc.; **48BL:** John Peterson, Peterson Architects; interior design: Judy Hallden Design; **48BR:** Interior design: Michael Finch and Daniel Nichols; **52T:** Grey Design Studio; **55T:** Missie Neville Crawford; **58T:** Design by Nursery Lines; **58B:** Architect: Halperin & Christ; interior design: Linda Applewhite; **60–61:** Brenco Designs; **64T:** Developer/builder: Tommy Mathews, Tony Adams, Randy Cohen, The St. Joe Co.; Donna Brooks and Shona Binkowski, Brooks Interior Design; **64B:** Ren Chandler, Dyna Contracting; **69B:** Celeste Lewis Architect; **70–71:** Emma Star Jensen; **72–73T:** Decorative painting by Lisa Bohm/Hermosa Design; **77:** Molly Luetkemeyer, M. Design Interiors; **78–79:** Pamela Pennington Studios; **80:** Doreen Leong; **81T:** Obie Bowman, architect; **82:** DeMattei Construction; interior design: Ann Bertelsen and Leanne Holder; **83:** Julie Atwood; **85TR:** Joe P. Carr, Texture Antiques; **90B:** Jim Davis; **91T:** Lorri Kershner, L. Kershner Design, www.lkershnerdesign.com; **91B:** Catherine Macfee & Associates Interior Design; **92TL:** Joe and Kalli Rivers Altieri; **92B:** Designer: William Gotlieb;

Markie Nelson Interior Design; **83T:** Architect: Arlo Braun & Associates; interior design: Steve Neuman, Interior Aesthetics, Ltd.; **95B:** Peter O. Whiteley; **96:** Catherine Macfee & Associates Interior Design; **97B:** Frank Clementi, Julie Smith, architects; **99T:** interior design: Richard Witzel & Associates; **102–103:** Royce Meyerott and Lee Bryant; **104:** Design: Sandra C. Watkins; paint color: Joan Osburn, Osburn Design, www.osburndesign.com; **105T:** Architect: Thomas Bollay; **105B:** Cornerstone Builders; **107T:** Architect: Paul Wanzer; interior design: Kim Munizza; **110T:** Ellen Slack, Interior Dimensions; **110B:** Architect: Fran Halperin, Halperin & Christ; **111T:** Levy Art & Architecture; Drew Maran Construction/Design; Sandra Slater Environments; **112–113:** Styling by Laura del Fava; **114T:** Erin and Brian Ruff; **114B:** Architect: Jerry Waters; **116T:** Christine Worboys; **116B:** Belinda Benson Interior Design; **117:** Sasha Emerson Levin; **118:** Brad and Katy Polvorosa/Neos; **119T:** Interior design: Carol A. Spong; **119B:** Becky Wright and Jean Tucker; **120T:** Bauer Interior Design; **122:** EDI Architecture; interior design: Pamela Pennington; **123B:** Architect: Charlotte Jensen & Associates.

Index

Page numbers in **boldface** refer to photographs.